# ROLLING WAVES

# McGRAW-HILL READING

# ROLLING WAVES

## Authors

Elizabeth Sulzby
   The University of Michigan

James Hoffman
   University of Texas at Austin

Charles Mangrum II
   University of Miami,
   Coral Gables, Florida

Jerome Niles
   Virginia Polytechnic Institute

Timothy Shanahan
   University of Illinois at Chicago

William H. Teale
   University of Texas at San Antonio

Arnold Webb
   Research for Better Schools
   Philadelphia, Pennsylvania

## Literature Consultant

Sylvia Peña
   University of Houston

## Contributing Authors

Lillian K. Boyd
   Detroit Public Schools

Bernard P. Floriani
   Delaware State Supervisor for Reading

Kay M. Kincade
   University of Oklahoma,
   Norman, Oklahoma

Jacqueline Kiraithe de Córdova
   California State University at Fullerton

Daniel R. Lawson
   Ambler Avenue Elementary School,
   Carson, California

Leon Lessinger, CEO
   Health Champions, Inc.
   Beverly Hills, California

George Mason
   University of Georgia

Kathleen Naylor
   Educational Consultant
   Brea, California

Karen S. Urbschat
   Wayne County Intermediate
   School District, Michigan

## McGraw-Hill School Division

New York     Oklahoma City     St. Louis     San Francisco     Dallas     Atlanta

The title of this book, "Rolling Waves," is taken from the story "The Mouse at the Seashore" by Arnold Lobel.

Cover Illustration: Roy Pendleton

Grateful acknowledgment for permission to reprint copyrighted material, illustrations and photographs appearing in this book is made on page 348 of this book, which is hereby made a part of this copyright page.

ISBN 0-07-042084-X

McGraw-Hill School Division
1200 Northwest 63rd Street
Oklahoma City, Oklahoma 73116-5712

3 4 5 6 7 8 9 0—8 9 7 6 5 4 3 2 1 0 9

# Contents

# Part One

# Builders

◇ Award-winning
book or author

# Part Two

# Dreamers

# Part Three

# Mysteries

◇ Award-winning
book or author

**8**

# Part Four    Ventures

# Reading on Your Own

The steps in this plan can help you read better.

**Before You Read**

- Read the name of the story.
- Look at the pictures.
- Think about what you will read in the story.
- Think about what you already know about this kind of story.

## As You Read

- Stop after every page.
- Think about what you have read so far.
- Think about what might come next.

Sometimes you may come to a word you don't know. Use these steps to understand the word.

1. Try saying the word out loud.
2. Read the words that come before and after the new word. They may give you a clue to the meaning of the new word.
3. Look up the word. Use the glossary at the back of the book, or use a dictionary.
4. Ask for help.

## After You Read

- Use your own words to retell what you have read.
- Think of the most important things you read.

# PART ONE

# Builders

What are you able to build with your blocks?
Castles and palaces, temples and docks.
Rain may keep raining, and others go roam,
But I can be happy and building at home.

from *Block City*
by Robert Louis Stevenson

◆

Building something can be fun. Whether you build
alone or with friends, whatever you make becomes
special because *you* have made it. The people you'll
read about in these stories all make or build
something special of their own. As you read, think:
What can you make when you are ready to build
something new?

13

# Exploring Words About Builders

### Starting with What You Know

When you think about builders, what ideas come to mind? The words in the box below tell about builders. Use these words and words of your own to answer the questions after the box.

| | | |
|---|---|---|
| houses | think | hammer |
| plan | wood | boats |
| nails | build | shape |

Many builders plan before they build anything. What else might a builder do? Builders use hammers to build things. What other tools might a builder use? Builders build houses. What else might a builder build?

### Building a Word Map

The word map shows how some of the words in the box above go together. Think about words you can add to the map. Use words from the box and other words of your own.

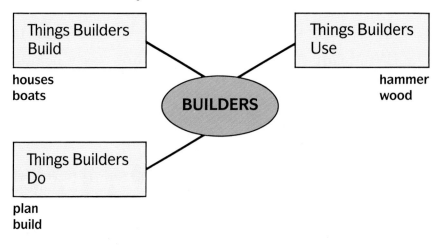

Things Builders Build
houses
boats

Things Builders Use
hammer
wood

BUILDERS

Things Builders Do
plan
build

## Finishing a Story

Look at the story below. The story tells about a girl who builds something. Some words are missing. Think of the words you would use to finish the story. Use the words from the box and word map in this lesson for ideas. Complete the story.

Joan wanted a treehouse. She began to _____. She had an idea. "I will _____ my own treehouse!" she decided. Joan knew she had to _____ carefully before she started.

First, she _____ a big tree. Then, she looked for some _____ to make the treehouse. She needed tools. She would use a _____ and a _____. Joan began to build.

Soon her _____ was done. How will Joan get the treehouse into the tree?

Share your story with your classmates. how were the stories different? What words did your classmates use?

## As You Read

In this part of the book, you will read about builders and the things they build. Keeping a Reader's Log will help you remember important thoughts, ideas, and words. As you read, make notes in your log. You could begin your Reader's Log with the word map. Add new words to the map as you find them.

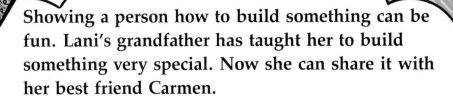

Showing a person how to build something can be fun. Lani's grandfather has taught her to build something very special. Now she can share it with her best friend Carmen.

# Sails in the Sky

◆

## by Laura Schenone

It is kite season now. That's what my friend Lani calls the fall—kite season. We go up to her roof every day to build kites. Her grandfather is teaching us how to make them the Chinese way, the way he learned when he was a boy.

If it wasn't for Lani and her grandfather I never would have known anything about kites. When I used to think about flying I would think of planes: loud engines and people in rows of seats with tiny windows. I would imagine flying to Puerto Rico, where my family is from. Now when I think of flying, I think of kites.

Lani and I got to be friends last year. We used to do things together after school. This year she seemed to be busy a lot. She would say she had to get right home when school was out. When I asked her why, she would just smile and say she was working on something with her grandfather.

One day Lani asked me to come home with her after school. She said she had something to show me. When we got to her apartment, we climbed six flights to the top of her building. Lani's grandfather was waiting for us on the roof. He was attaching a string to a beautiful kite—a Chinese hawk that he and Lani had built.

"So now you know what I've been doing after school," Lani said.

Lani's grandfather showed us the kites he had built. There was a butterfly kite, a fish kite, and bird kites for all kinds of wind. The kite he was most proud of was his dragon kite. It had a long tail made of many round pieces he had strung together and painted green and red. I really hope that someday I can see that dragon kite fly. I would like to see that long tail twist through the air. Lani's grandfather said it is very difficult. It needs a lot of wind and many people. I asked if Lani and I could help him fly it. He said, "We'll see."

"Do you want to help me get the hawk into the air, Carmen?" Lani asked. When I said yes she gave me the kite to hold. Then she stood a few feet away with the string. When the wind came I let go and she pulled the string tighter and tighter until the kite lifted up into the sky above the city.

Now Lani and I are both making bird kites. I will paint mine blue when it is finished. It is a small bird with a light spine for light wind.

When we finish our kites, we will take them to the park. Or we will just fly them up here on the roof with Lani's grandfather.

To me the best way to fly is not in an airplane, but with a kite. I can feel the wind in my arms when I hold the string. I can't wait until my own kite is finished. I will make it twist and dive. I will watch the blue wings that I painted lift higher and higher into the air. It will be like my own small sail in the sky.

## Thinking About the Theme

1. Carmen loved to fly the kites that Lani and Lani's grandfather made. How do you think she'll like it when she flies a kite she made herself?

2. If you were making your own kite, what would it look like? What other things might you like to make or build on your own?

# Understanding Order in Stories

What did Randy do first? What did he make?

## Thinking About Order

In real life, things happen in **order**. We put food in our mouths, chew it, and then swallow it. What other things happen in order?

Sometimes writers give clues about the order in stories. They use words such as *first*, *next*, *then*, and *finally*. Read the paragraph. Tell what happened in order.

> Randy wanted to make a bed for his kitten. First he went to his room. Then he found a shoe box and an old T-shirt. Next he cut a hole in the box. Finally, he folded the shirt to fit inside the box.

In the paragraph, Randy first went to his room. Then he got the box and the shirt. Next he cut a hole in the box, and finally he put the shirt inside the box.

Sometimes a story does not have clue words. You must use what you already know to tell the order. Think carefully as you read.

## Practice

Read the paragraph. Tell the order in which things happened. Tell the story again, and add clue words to show the order.

The plane landed at the airport. Ann and her mother got off the plane and saw Uncle Irving waiting for them. Uncle Irving drove Ann and her mother to his house. He showed them his garden and the greenhouse he had made.

## As You Read

Look for clue words, such as *first, next, then,* and *finally.* If there are no clue words, use what you already know and ask yourself these questions:

- What happened first?
- What happened next?
- What happened then?
- What happened finally?

Apply what you know about order in stories as you read the two selections that follow. Use the side notes to help you.

When a big orange splot spills on Mr. Plumbean's roof, his neighbors wait for him to paint it. But Mr. Plumbean has a better idea.

# THE BIG ORANGE SPLOT

by Daniel Manus Pinkwater

Mr. Plumbean lived on a street where all the houses were the same.

He liked it that way. So did everybody else on Mr. Plumbean's street. "This is a neat street," they would say. Then one day . . .

A seagull flew over Mr. Plumbean's house. He was carrying a can of bright orange paint. (No one knows why.) And he dropped the can (no one knows why) right over Mr. Plumbean's house.

It made a big orange splot on Mr. Plumbean's house.

"Ooooh! Too bad!" everybody said.
"Mr. Plumbean will have to paint his house again."

First the street is neat. Notice the clue word then.

**23**

"I suppose I will," said Mr. Plumbean. But he didn't paint his house right away. He looked at the big orange splot for a long time; then he went about his business.

The neighbors got tired of seeing that big orange splot. Someone said, "Mr. Plumbean, we wish you would get around to painting your house."

"O.K.," said Mr. Plumbean.

First, he got some blue paint and some white paint. Then that night he got busy. He painted at night because it was cooler.

When the paint was gone, the roof was blue. The walls were white. And the big orange splot was still there.

Then he got some more paint. He got red paint, yellow paint, green paint, and purple paint.

In the morning the other people on the street came out of their houses. Their houses were all the same. But Mr. Plumbean's house was like a rainbow. It was like a tropical island. It was like an explosion.

Something is happening. The clue words show the order.

Think about what will happen next.

There was the big orange splot. And there were
little orange splots. There were purple stripes.
There were pictures of elephants and lions and
pretty girls and steamshovels.

The people said, "Plumbean has popped his
cork, flipped his wig, blown his stack, and
dropped his stopper." They went away muttering.

That day Mr. Plumbean bought carpenter's tools.
That night he built a tower on top of his roof, and
he painted a clock on the tower.

The next day the people said, "Plumbean has
gushed his mush, lost his marbles, and slipped his
hawser." They decided they would pretend not to
notice.

These things
happen in order.

**25**

Mr. Plumbean does things in order.

That very night Mr. Plumbean got a truck full of green things. He planted palm trees, baobabs, thorn bushes, and frangipani. In the morning he bought a hammock and an alligator.

When the other people came out of their houses, they saw Mr. Plumbean swinging in a hammock between two palm trees. They saw an alligator lying in the grass. Mr. Plumbean was drinking lemonade.

"Plumbean has gone too far!"

"This used to be a neat street!"

"Plumbean, what have you done to your house?" the people shouted.

"My house is me and I am it. My house is where I like to be and it looks like all my dreams," Mr. Plumbean said.

The people went away. They asked the man who lived next door to Mr. Plumbean to go and have a talk with him. "Tell him that we all liked it here before he changed his house. Tell him that his house has to be the same as ours so we can have a neat street."

Think about what will happen next.

**26**

The man went to see Mr. Plumbean that evening. They sat between the palm trees drinking lemonade and talking all night long.

Early the next morning the man went out to get lumber and rope and nails and paint. When the people came out of their houses they saw a red and yellow ship next door to the house of Mr. Plumbean.

The neighbor does things in order, too.

"What have you done to your house?" they shouted at the man.

"My house is me and I am it. My house is where I like to be and it looks like all my dreams," said the man, who had always loved ships.

"He's just like Plumbean!" the people said. "He's got bees in his bonnet, bats in his belfry, and knots in his noodle!"

Then, one by one, they went to see Mr. Plumbean, late at night. They would sit under the palm trees and drink lemonade and talk about their dreams— and whenever anybody visited Mr. Plumbean's house, the very next day that person would set about changing his own house to fit his dreams.

Whenever a stranger came to the street of Mr. Plumbean and his neighbors, the stranger would say, "This is not a neat street."

Then all the people would say, "Our street is us and we are it. Our street is where we like to be, and it looks like all our dreams."

*Everyone began to like Mr. Plumbean's idea.*

## A Reader Says

*I think if this really happened, people would love to visit the street and look at all the different houses.*

How did you feel about the story?

# After You Read

## Thinking About What You Read

**1.** Why didn't Mr. Plumbean paint his house neatly right after the splot appeared?

**2.** What gave Plumbean the idea of building onto his house and painting it like a rainbow?

**3.** How might Plumbean have persuaded his neighbors to paint their houses?

**4.** Why did the people say their houses looked like their dreams?

## Thinking About How You Read

How did understanding the order in which things happened help you understand how the street changed?

## Sharing and Listening

Compare the reasons why people liked their street both before and after they painted their houses. Listen carefully as other people give their ideas.

## Writing

Pretend that you are the seagull and that you are talking to Mr. Plumbean. Write a few sentences telling him why you dropped the paint on his house. Write what Mr. Plumbean might say to you.

No matter what you do or make, your muscles are working. In this article, you can find out how muscles work.

# MUSCLES AT WORK

by Lee Hoyt

Don't move a muscle!

That is one direction no one can follow. No matter how quiet and still you try to be, muscles are always moving in your body. Muscles are always moving your rib cage up and down so you can breathe. If you are standing still, the muscles that pull on your bones are moving so you can keep your balance. Even when you're asleep, your heart muscle is working to pump blood and the muscles that let your blood move through your body are at work.

Each person has more than six hundred muscles. A new baby has as many as a baseball player. One hundred of the muscles are in your face and neck alone, letting you laugh, close your eyes, read, and eat food.

Some of your muscles are called skeletal muscles. They are fastened to bones. The biceps muscle is fastened to your lower arm bone, near your elbow. It runs along your upper arm and is fastened at the top to a bone in your shoulder. When you bend your elbow, the biceps contracts, or gets shorter and firmer. If you press your upper arm while you are bending your elbow, you can feel the biceps as it pulls up your lower arm.

When you stretch your arm out again, you use a different muscle, the triceps. It pulls your arm back down.

A muscle can pull, but not push. So muscles often work in pairs. The biceps and triceps work as partners. They take turns pulling when you bend and straighten your elbow. Many other muscles work together in pairs, such as the muscles that open and close your mouth.

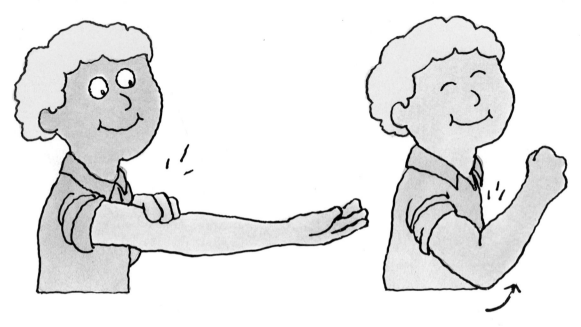

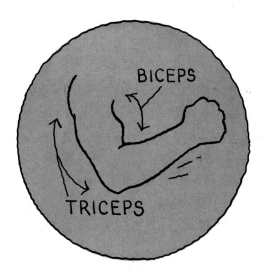

Because of your skeletal muscles, you can walk, jump, stretch, draw pictures, and do hundreds of other things every day.

You have other muscles called smooth muscles. They work without your thinking about them. There are smooth muscles in your eyes that change the size of your pupils. When you first go outside on a bright day, the pupil, or black opening in your eye, gets smaller because the eye doesn't need so much light. When you go into a dark room, your eye needs more light and the pupil gets larger. Two sets of smooth muscles work in each eye to make the pupil larger or smaller. Like the biceps and triceps, these two sets of eye muscles work together.

Other smooth muscles help your body make use of the food you eat, and help the blood move through your body. The smooth muscles keep your body running well, even though you may not think about them, or even know that they are at work.

The heart is an important smooth muscle. No other muscle is exactly like it. Like the muscles you use to breathe, it never stops working. Day and night it is busy pumping blood. Your heart never gets tired because it takes a quick rest after each heartbeat.

Skeletal muscles need a longer rest after they've been working hard. If they get too tired, they will stop working for a short time. If you hold something heavy for a long time, sooner or later you may have to let go of it because the skeletal muscles in your arm and hand will need to rest.

When muscles are not used enough, they get small and weak. After a broken arm or leg has been in a cast for a month or two, it will feel very weak because its muscles have not been used. The arm or leg will need to stretch and exercise for a little while before it can be strong again.

Muscles become strong through exercise. Without exercise, a tiny baby could never grow up to be a strong baseball player. First the baby exercises by kicking and wiggling for many months. When it grows strong enough to crawl, it exercises even more. At last it is able to pull itself up, stand alone, and take a step or two. Three hundred of its muscles must work together for the baby to take just one step. No wonder a baby falls down many times as it is learning to walk. But each time the baby pulls itself up again, it is using its muscles to grow stronger.

Muscles that are used a lot become big and strong. Someone who lifts heavy things all day will have big biceps. A bike rider will get strong leg muscles. The muscles that you use most will become the strongest.

Each of your muscles works for you in its special way, even though you may not notice it or think about it. Your muscles are always moving.

## A Reader Says

*Exercise is important. I'm going to practice my push-ups so that my biceps get stronger!*

How did you feel about the article?

# After You Read

## Thinking About What You Read

**1.** Which kinds of activities would make only a few muscles work? Which would make most muscles work?

**2.** How are smooth muscles and skeletal muscles alike? How are they different?

**3.** Why do muscles need both exercise and rest?

**4.** Would it be possible to exercise smooth muscles as well as skeletal muscles? Why or why not?

## Thinking About How You Read

How did looking for clue words help you know the order in which a baby learns to use muscles?

## Sharing and Listening

Tell how the body builds muscles. Tell how people begin to build muscles as soon as they are born. Listen carefully as other people share their ideas.

## Writing

Write a few sentences telling what kinds of exercises or sports you enjoy. Then explain which muscles you are building by doing those exercises or sports.

STRATEGY
◄BUILDER►

for **Do You Have the Time, Lydia**?
and **The Patchwork Quilt**

# Understanding Stories That Seem Real

### Starting with What You Know

You know that some stories could never really happen. Other stories seem as if they really could happen. These kinds of stories are **realistic**. Which of the two kinds of stories do you like best? Tell why.

### Thinking About Realistic Stories

Realistic stories have the same parts that all stories have.

Characters: These are the people in the story.

Setting: This is the place where the story happens.

Plot: These are the main events in the story. In some stories, two or three events make up the plot.

Outcome: This is the way the story ends. In many stories, the main character solves a problem.

In a realistic story, the characters seem like real people. The setting seems like a real place. The events that make up the plot seem as if they could really happen. In the outcome, a character seems to really solve a problem, and does so in a way that could really happen.

**Before You Read**

Look at the name of the story and look at the pictures. Try to guess what will happen in the story.

**As You Read**

Stop after every big event or after you meet a new character. Think about what you have read so far. Try to guess what will happen next. Ask yourself these questions. The questions with blue diamonds are for any kind of story. The questions with red diamonds are for realistic stories.

Characters: ◆ Who are the characters?
◆ How do they seem like real people?

Setting: ◆ Where does the story happen?
◆ How does the place seem real?

Plot: ◆ What is happening in the story?
◆ How do the events seem real?

Outcome: ◆ How does the story end?
◆ What problem does the character solve?

Apply what you know about realistic stories as you read the two realistic stories that follow. Use the side notes to help you.

**Lydia loves to build and make things. If only she had the time to finish what she starts! How can her brother help her understand that sometimes it's best to take the time?**

# Do You Have the Time, Lydia?

## by Evaline Ness

These are the characters. The setting is also described here.

Once there was a little girl named Lydia. She lived with her father, who was a florist, and Andy, who was her brother. Their house was on a tropical island in a warm and noisy sea.

Every day Lydia's father was busy in his greenhouse, where the plants and flowers grew so tall they needed holes in the roof to breathe.

Every day Lydia was busy painting pictures, reading books, hammering nails, gathering shells, sewing clothes, and baking cakes. Lydia was so busy doing so *many* things, she left things unfinished—she never finished *any*thing.

Some real people act this way.

Andy didn't do anything because he didn't know how to. If he asked Lydia to help him do something, she always said: *No, no, no, no! I haven't got time!*

Whenever her father heard Lydia say: *No, no, no, no! I haven't got time!* he always said, "Oh no? Oh ho! If you *take* time you can *have* time."

But Lydia was too busy to listen.

Lydia's father sounds like a real parent.

**41**

One bright and early morning, as Andy splashed along the beach, he found an empty lobster trap. He dragged it home and into Lydia's room, where she sat sewing a dress for the cat.

"Look," he shouted, "a racing car! Please, oh please, Lydia, fix it for me so I can be in Dr. Arnold's race! The prize is a dog!"

Without looking up, Lydia said, "No, no, no, no! I haven't got time!"

"The race is this afternoon!" pleaded Andy.

Lydia stopped sewing long enough to look at the lobster trap.

"Well, all right. I'll fix it. But later."

"You don't *care*!" cried Andy.

"I *said* I'd fix it, didn't I?"

Think about what will happen next.

Andy looked at Lydia for a long time. Then, slowly, he backed out of the room.

Lydia dropped the cat's dress. She found her roller skates and pulled them apart. She tied each skate half to the four corners of the trap. Then she cut two large paper headlights and glued them to the front. She took her box full of doll's clothes, dumped everything in it onto the floor, and placed it in the trap for a driver's seat.

Lydia begins to build something. She does things that a real person might do.

"Perfect!" said Lydia. "All it needs is a steering wheel, and I know just where to find one!"

Lydia ran to the garage. In one corner, on a table, was a pile of junk. At the very top was a doll stroller with one wheel. As Lydia started to climb on the table, she noticed a large glass bowl on the floor.

Think about what will happen next.

**43**

"All *that* needs," muttered Lydia, "is a little water and a few tiny fish. And I know just where to find them!"

Away Lydia raced. She whizzed through the pine grove and down to the boathouse to get her fishing net.

Notice how many new things Lydia starts to do.

The first thing she saw there was her father's boat filled halfway with water. Lydia tried to tip over the boat. It wouldn't budge. She found a rusty can in the boathouse and started to dip out the water. But the more she dipped, the more water seeped in. Lydia threw the can away and fled up the beach to the greenhouse to tell her father.

Halfway there she stopped. At the water's edge she spotted a pearly gray sea gull. His eyes were closed and one wing was bent crookedly beneath him. Just as Lydia stooped to touch him, he opened his eyes. Suddenly he shrieked and slapped her face with his good wing. Lydia backed off.

"You need a doctor," shouted Lydia, "and I know just where to find one!"

She began to run. She ran so fast she had run out of breath by the time she reached Dr. Arnold's house. But Dr. Arnold wasn't home. Attached to the door knocker was a note: BACK IN 10 MINUTES. JUDGING RACE.

The race!

Up the street flew Lydia. At the top of the hill she came to a sudden halt. There stood Andy, alone. The race was over. All the cars were at the bottom of the hill and Dr. Arnold was just giving a spotted dog to the winner.

Andy looked at Lydia with big tears in his eyes. Then he turned and fled.

"Andy!" cried Lydia. "I was fixing it but I didn't have enough time!"

Andy kept running. He didn't look back.

Lydia watched him until he turned a corner. Then she walked back to Dr. Arnold's house. She sat down on the steps and cried and cried. Then she stopped, because she had no tears left.

Lydia's actions make Andy feel bad.

Suddenly a voice said, "Well! Have you finished your crying?"

Lydia looked down and saw Dr. Arnold's shoes, then she looked up and saw Dr. Arnold's face. Between two sniffs Lydia said, "At least I finally took time to finish *something*."

Think about how Lydia feels.

Dr. Arnold patted Lydia's head.

"*Now* what?" he asked.

Then Lydia remembered the sea gull.

"The sea gull!" she shouted. "Dr. Arnold! It's hurt itself. It's on the beach, and it can't fly!"

"Hurry!" she cried, when Dr. Arnold went into his office to get his little black bag.

"Hurry!" she called, as she ran ahead to the beach.

At last they were there, and there was the sea gull.

Very carefully Dr. Arnold worked a pill down the gull's throat to make it sleep.   Then he taped its broken wing.

"This bird is going to be just fine," said Dr. Arnold, "but it won't be able to fly for a few days. Why don't you take the gull home, Lydia, and feed it a nice fat fish when it wakes up. That is, if you have enough time."

Lydia makes up her mind to take the time to help the sea gull.

Lydia looked down at the sleeping sea gull. "Oh ho! I'll *take* time!" said Lydia.

After Dr. Arnold left, Lydia carried the gull home.

She lined the bottom of a basket with seaweed. Then she carefully laid the gull on its cool wet bed.

Lydia went looking for Andy. She found him under the porch.

Lydia brought the sea gull in its basket and placed it in front of Andy.

"Andy," said Lydia, "look what I found for you. It will be real when it wakes up. You can have it all for your own."

Andy looked at the gull. He said nothing.

"Did you know that dogs can't fly?" asked Lydia.

Without looking at Lydia, Andy said, "I don't want your old bird."

Lydia left the sea gull with Andy and went back to the garage. She climbed on the table and pulled the wheel off the stroller. As she was leaving the garage, Lydia spotted a birdhouse that she had started to make a long time ago. All it needed was a roof.

"What that birdhouse needs . . ." began Lydia. She stopped and looked at the wheel in her hand, ". . . is *nothing!*"

Think about what will happen next.

Lydia shot out of the garage and into the house to her room.

She had just finished fixing the wheel into place when a voice at her shoulder said: "I don't want your old trap."

Lydia seems to have changed the way she acts.

"Oh, Andy!" pleaded Lydia. "Yes you do too! I'll paint it red and put a bell on it and it will be a fire engine and you can go all around town and pretend to put out fires and help people!"

There was a long silence.

"Will it have a ladder?" asked Andy.

"Yes, a ladder too! I promise! I promise!"

"But you don't have enough time," said Andy.

"Oh no? Oh ho! If I *take* time I can *have* time!" said Lydia.

## A Reader Says

*Lydia was only trying to help Andy. Maybe he should have built his own car!*

How did you feel about the story?

# After You Read

## Thinking About What You Read

**1.** Why did Lydia try to do so many things at once?

**2.** Did Andy really expect Lydia to finish his car in time? How did he feel about Lydia after the race?

**3.** Do you think Lydia would have remembered about the race if she hadn't needed Dr. Arnold?

**4.** How did Lydia feel about herself when the race was over and she saw her brother?

## Thinking About How You Read

How did knowing that this story was realistic help you guess how Lydia would solve her problem?

## Sharing and Listening

Tell what you liked or disliked about Lydia. Why? Tell how Lydia could have helped Andy. Tell whether you think Andy could have helped Lydia. Listen as others give their opinions.

## Writing

Imagine you are Lydia. Write a few sentences in your diary about why it is good to take the time to finish something you start.

# Building a Bird Feeder

You have just read a story about Lydia, a girl who liked to build things. Lydia started to build a birdhouse but didn't finish it. A birdhouse might be hard to finish, but a bird feeder is something you can make easily if you follow these directions.

**1.** All you need to start with is an old aluminum pie pan and some sturdy string or twine. Ask a parent or an older friend to punch four holes around the rim of the pie pan.

**2.** Cut four pieces of string, each about three feet long. Make a knot at the end of each piece, then thread each one through one of the holes. The knot should be underneath, so that the string doesn't slip out.

**3.** Tie the four pieces together at the other end. Make sure to save a small piece of string to tie to the top, so that you will have a loop for hanging your feeder.

Now you are ready to hang the feeder in a place where birds can find it. If there is a tree or a large bush nearby, hang it from a low branch. If not, ask a parent or an older friend to nail a narrow piece of wood to a window frame, and hang the feeder there.

Once the feeder is in place, you'll need to fill it. Here are some kinds of food your bird visitors might like.

**1.** Birds love seeds, so put a good supply of them in your feeder. You can buy bags of birdseed in many grocery stores or at a pet store.

**2.** Peanut butter and suet are very good in winter. Suet is animal fat and, like peanut butter, it gives birds extra energy. You can buy suet at a pet store.

**3.** Some birds like fruit. Put half an orange, some apple slices, or a handful of raisins into the feeder. Many birds might also like to eat some leftover table scraps. Try putting out some bits of egg, toast, lettuce, or potatoes.

When your feeder is in place and filled with food, you will be ready for your visitors.

When Tanya's grandmother makes her quilt, each
old scrap is important. She and Tanya work
together to take the old cloth and make something
new and beautiful.

# ❖THE❖
# PATCHWORK
# QUILT

## by Valerie Flournoy

Tanya sat restlessly on her chair by the kitchen
window. For several days she had had to stay in
bed with a cold. But now Tanya's cold was almost
gone. She wanted to go outside and enjoy the fresh
air and the arrival of spring.

"Mama, when can I go outside?" asked Tanya.
Mama pulled the tray of biscuits from the oven and
placed it on the counter.

"In time," she murmured. "All in good time."

"I'm going to talk to Grandma," Tanya said.

Grandma was sitting in her favorite spot—the big
soft chair in front of the picture window. In her lap
were scraps of materials of all sizes and colors.
Tanya recognized some of them. The purple plaid
was from Papa's old work shirt, and the red scraps
were from the shirt Ted had torn that winter.

"What are you going to do with all that stuff?" Tanya asked.

"Stuff? This isn't stuff. These little pieces are going to make a quilt, a patchwork quilt."

Tanya tilted her head. "I know what a quilt is, Grandma. There's one on your bed, but it's old and dirty and Mama can never get it clean."

Grandma sighed. "It's not dirty, baby. It's worn, the way it's supposed to be. My mother made me a quilt when I wasn't any older than you. But sometimes we forget the old ways."

Tanya leaned on the chair and rested her head on her grandmother's shoulder.

Just then Mama walked in with two glasses of milk and some biscuits. Mama looked at the scraps of material that were scattered all over. "Grandma," she said, "I just cleaned this room, and now it's a mess."

"It's not a mess, Mama," Tanya said through a mouthful of biscuits. "It's a quilt."

"A quilt! You don't need these scraps. I can get you a quilt," Mama said.

Grandma looked at her daughter and then turned to her grandchild. "Yes, your mama can get you a quilt from the store. But it won't be like my patchwork quilt, and it won't last as long either."

Mama looked at Grandma, then picked up Tanya's empty glass and went to make lunch.

"Grandma, I'll help you make your quilt," Tanya said. "If we start now we'll be done in no time!"

Grandma held Tanya close and patted her head.
"It's going to take quite a while to make this quilt,
not a few days or a week—not even a month. A
good quilt, a masterpiece . . ." Grandma's eyes
shone. "Why I need more material. More gold and
blue, some red and green. And I'll need the time
to do it right. It'll take a year at least."

"A year," shouted Tanya. "That's too long. I can't wait that long, Grandma."

Grandma laughed. "A year's not that long, baby. Making this quilt is going to be a joy. Now run along and let Grandma rest." She turned her head to the sunlight and closed her eyes.

"I'm going to make a masterpiece," she murmured, clutching a scrap of cloth in her hand.

The arrival of fall meant school and Halloween. This year Tanya would be an African princess. She danced around in the long, flowing robes Mama had made from several yards of colorful material. Grandma cut some squares out of the leftover scraps and added Tanya to the quilt too!

The days grew colder but Tanya and her brothers didn't mind. They knew snow wasn't far away. Mama dreaded winter's coming. Every year she would plead with Grandma to move away from the drafty window, but Grandma wouldn't budge.

It was the end of November when Ted, Jim, and Tanya got their wish. They awoke one morning to find everything in sight covered with snow. Tanya got dressed and flew down the stairs. Ted and Jim, and even Mama and Papa, were already outside.

The family spent the morning and most of the afternoon sledding down the hill. Finally, when they were all numb from the cold, they went inside for hot chocolate and sandwiches.

"I think I'll go talk to Grandma," Mama said.

"Then she can explain to you about our quilt—our very own family quilt," Tanya said.

Mama saw the glint in her youngest child's eyes.

"Why, I may just have her do that, young lady," Mama said as she walked out of the kitchen.

Tanya leaned over the table to see into the living room. Grandma was hunched over, her eyes close to the material as she made tiny stitches. Mama sat at the old woman's feet. Tanya couldn't hear what was said but she knew Grandma was telling Mama all about quilts and how *this* quilt would be very special. Tanya sipped her chocolate slowly, then she saw Mama pick up a piece of material, rub it with her fingers, and smile.

From then on Mama and Grandma spent their winter nights working on the quilt. Mama did the sewing while Grandma cut the material and placed the scraps in a pattern of colors. Even while they were cooking and baking all their Christmas specialties during the day, at night they still worked on the quilt. Only once did Mama put it aside. She wanted to wear something special Christmas night, so she bought some gold material and made a beautiful dress. Tanya knew without asking that the gold scraps would be in the quilt too.

There was much singing and laughing that Christmas. All Grandma's children and grandchildren and nieces and nephews came to pay their respects. The Christmas tree lights shone brightly, filling the room with sparkling colors. Later, when everyone had gone home, Papa said he had never felt so much happiness in the house. And Mama agreed.

When Tanya got downstairs the next morning, she found Papa fixing pancakes.

"Where's Mama?" asked Tanya.

"Grandma doesn't feel well," Papa said. "Your mother is with her now till the doctor gets here."

"Will Grandma be all right?" Ted asked.

Papa rubbed Ted's head and smiled. "There's nothing for you to worry about. We'll take care of Grandma."

Tanya looked into the living room. There on the back of the big chair rested the patchwork quilt. It was folded neatly, just as Grandma had left it.

"Mother didn't want us to know she wasn't feeling well. She thought it would spoil our Christmas," Mama told them later, her face drawn and tired, her eyes a puffy red. "Now it's up to all of us to be quiet and get her whatever she needs." Papa put an arm around Mama's shoulder.

"Can we see Grandma?" Tanya asked.

"No, not tonight," Papa said. "Grandma needs plenty of rest."

It was the day before New Year's before the children were finally permitted to see their grandmother. She looked tired and spoke in whispers.

"We miss you, Grandma," Ted said.

"And your muffins and hot chocolate," added Jim. Grandma smiled.

"Your quilt misses you too, Grandma," Tanya said. Grandma's smile faded from her lips. Her eyes grew cloudy.

"My masterpiece," Grandma sighed. "It would have been beautiful. Almost half finished." She closed her eyes and turned away from her grandchildren. Papa whispered it was time to leave.

Tanya walked slowly to where the quilt lay. She had seen Grandma and Mama work on it. Tanya thought real hard. She knew how to cut the scraps with the scissors, but she wasn't sure of the rest. Just then Tanya felt a hand resting on her shoulder. She looked up and saw Mama.

"Tomorrow," Mama said.

New Year's Day was the beginning. After dinner, Tanya and Mama looked carefully at the quilt.

"You cut more squares, Tanya, while I stitch some patches together," Mama said.

Tanya snipped and trimmed the scraps of material. Mama watched her carefully, making sure the squares were all the same size. Often, when Mama had to look after Grandma, Tanya worked by herself. Then one night, as Papa read them stories, Jim walked over and looked at the quilt. In it he saw patches from his old blue jeans. Without saying a word Jim picked up the scissors and some scraps and started to make squares. Ted helped Jim put the squares in piles while Mama showed Tanya how to join them.

Every day, as soon as she got home from school, Tanya worked on the quilt. Ted and Jim were too busy with sports, and Mama was looking after Grandma, so Tanya worked alone. But after a few weeks she stopped. Something was wrong—something was missing, Tanya thought. For days the quilt lay on the back of the chair. No one knew why Tanya had stopped working. Tanya would sit and look at the quilt. Finally she knew. Some*thing* wasn't missing. Some*one* was missing from the quilt.

That night before she went to bed Tanya tiptoed into Grandma's room, a pair of scissors in her hand. She quietly lifted the end of Grandma's old quilt and carefully removed a few squares.

February and March came and went as Mama proudly watched her daughter work on the last few rows of patches. Tanya always found time for the quilt. Grandma had been watching too. She had been getting stronger as the months passed. Soon she was able to sit in her chair by the window. She would hum softly to herself and watch Tanya work.

Summer was almost here. One June day Tanya came home to find Grandma working on the quilt again! She had finished sewing the last few squares together; the stuffing was in place and she was already pinning on the backing.

"Grandma!" Tanya shouted.

Grandma looked up. "Hush, child. It's almost time to do the quilting on these patches. But first I have some special finishing touches. . . ."

The next night Grandma cut the last thread with her teeth. "There. It's done," she said. Mama helped Grandma spread out the quilt.

Nobody had realized how big it had gotten or how beautiful. Reds, greens, blues, and golds, light shades and dark, blended in and out.

"It's beautiful," Papa said. He touched the gold patch, looked at Mama, and remembered. Jim remembered too. There was his blue and the red from Ted's shirt. There was Tanya's Halloween costume. And there was Grandma. Even though her patch was old, it blended right in.

They all remembered the past year. They especially remembered Tanya and all her work. So it had been decided. In the right hand corner of the last row of patches was delicately stitched, "For Tanya from your Mama and Grandma."

## A Reader Says

*I think Tanya helped her Grandmother get well by not giving up on finishing the quilt.*

How did you feel about the story?

# After You Read

## Thinking About What You Read

**1.** Why did Grandma say her own quilt was worn, the way it was supposed to be?

**2.** How did Tanya feel about the quilt at first? How did her feelings change?

**3.** In what ways was the quilt a family quilt?

**4.** What might have happened if Tanya hadn't worked on the quilt during the time Grandma was sick?

## Thinking About How You Read

How did knowing that this story was realistic help you understand how Tanya and her family would act?

## Sharing and Listening

Tell if you think Tanya's quilt was more beautiful than a quilt you could buy in the store. Why or why not? Listen carefully as other people tell what they think.

## Writing

Is there something that you would like to make by yourself? Write a few sentences that tell what it is and why you want to make it.

Pooh and Piglet want to build a house for Eeyore.
They surprise their friend in a way they never
imagined.

# *In Which*
# A House Is Built
# at Pooh Corner
# for Eeyore

◆

### by A. A. Milne

One day when Pooh Bear had nothing else to do, he thought he would do something, so he went round to Piglet's house to see what Piglet was doing. It was still snowing as he stumped over the white forest track, and he expected to find Piglet warming his toes in front of his fire, but to his surprise he saw that the door was open, and the more he looked inside the more Piglet wasn't there.

"He's out," said Pooh sadly. "That's what it is. He's not in. I shall have to go a fast Thinking Walk by myself. Bother!"

But first he thought that he would knock very loudly just to make *quite* sure . . . and while he waited for Piglet not to answer, he jumped up and down to keep warm, and a hum came suddenly into his head, which seemed to him a Good Hum, such as is Hummed Hopefully to Others.

The more it snows
  (Tiddely pom),
The more it goes
  (Tiddely pom),
The more it goes
  (Tiddely pom),
On snowing.

And nobody knows
　　(Tiddely pom),
How cold my toes
　　(Tiddely pom),
How cold my toes
　　(Tiddely pom),
Are growing.

"So what I'll do," said Pooh, "is I'll do this. I'll just go home first and see what the time is, and perhaps I'll put a muffler round my neck, and then I'll go and see Eeyore and sing it to him."

He hurried back to his own house; and his mind was so busy on the way with the hum that he was getting ready for Eeyore that, when he suddenly saw Piglet sitting in his best arm-chair, he could only stand there rubbing his head and wondering whose house he was in.

"Hallo, Piglet," he said. "I thought you were out."

"No," said Piglet, "it's you who were out, Pooh."

"So it was," said Pooh. "I knew one of us was."

He looked up at his clock, which had stopped at five minutes to eleven some weeks ago.

"Nearly eleven o'clock," said Pooh happily. "You're just in time for a little smackerel of something," and he put his head into the cupboard. "And then we'll go out, Piglet, and sing my song to Eeyore."

"Which song, Pooh?"

"The one we're going to sing to Eeyore," explained Pooh.

The clock was still saying five minutes to eleven when Pooh and Piglet set out on their way half an hour later. The wind had dropped, and the snow, tired of rushing round in circles trying to catch itself up, now fluttered gently down until it found a place on which to rest, and sometimes the place was Pooh's nose and sometimes it wasn't, and in a little while Piglet was wearing a white muffler round his neck and feeling more snowy behind the ears than he had ever felt before.

"Pooh," he said at last, and a little timidly, because he didn't want Pooh to think he was Giving In, "I was just wondering. How would it be if we went home now and *practised* your song, and then sang it to Eeyore to-morrow—or—or the next day, when we happen to see him."

"That's a very good idea, Piglet," said Pooh. "We'll practise it now as we go along. But it's no good going home to practise it, because it's a special Outdoor Song which Has To Be Sung In The Snow."

"Are you sure?" asked Piglet anxiously.

"Well, you'll see, Piglet, when you listen. Because this is how it begins. *The more it snows, tiddely pom—*"

"Tiddely what?" said Piglet.

"Pom," said Pooh. "I put that in to make it more hummy. *The more it goes, tiddely pom, the more—*"

"Didn't you say snows?"

"Yes, but that was *before*."

"Before the tiddely pom?"

"It was a *different* tiddely pom," said Pooh, feeling rather muddled now. "I'll sing it to you properly and then you'll see."

So he sang it again.

The more it
SNOWS-tiddely-pom,
The more it
GOES-tiddely-pom
The more it
GOES-tiddely-pom
On
Snowing.

And nobody
KNOWS-tiddely-pom,
How cold my
TOES-tiddely-pom
How cold my
TOES-tiddely-pom
Are
Growing.

He sang it like that, which is much the best way of singing it, and when he had finished, he waited for Piglet to say that, of all the Outdoor Hums for Snowy Weather he had ever heard, this was the best. And, after thinking the matter out carefully, Piglet said:

"Pooh," he said solemnly, "it isn't the *toes* so much as the *ears*."

By this time they were getting near Eeyore's Gloomy Place, which was where he lived, and as it was still very snowy behind Piglet's ears, and he was getting tired of it, they turned into a little pine wood, and sat down on the gate which led into it. They were out of the snow now, but it was very cold, and to keep themselves warm they sang Pooh's song right through six times, Piglet doing the tiddely-poms and Pooh doing the rest of it, and both of them thumping on the top of the gate with pieces of stick at the proper places. And in a little while they felt much warmer, and were able to talk again.

"I've been thinking," said Pooh, "and what I've been thinking is this. I've been thinking about Eeyore."

"What about Eeyore?"

"Well, poor Eeyore has nowhere to live."

"Nor he has," said Piglet.

"*You* have a house, Piglet, and I have a house, and they are very good houses. And Christopher Robin has a house, and Owl and Kanga and Rabbit have houses, and even Rabbit's friends and relations have houses or somethings, but poor Eeyore has nothing. So what I've been thinking is: Let's build him a house."

"That," said Piglet, "is a Grand Idea. Where shall we build it?"

"We will build it here," said Pooh, "just by this wood, out of the wind, because this is where I thought of it. And we will call this Pooh Corner. And we will build an Eeyore House with sticks at Pooh Corner for Eeyore."

"There was a heap of sticks on the other side of the wood," said Piglet. "I saw them. Lots and lots. All piled up."

"Thank you, Piglet," said Pooh. "What you have just said will be a Great Help to us, and because of it I could call this place Poohanpiglet Corner if Pooh Corner didn't sound better, which it does, being smaller and more like a corner. Come along."

So they got down off the gate and went around to the other side of the wood to fetch the sticks.

Christopher Robin had spent the morning indoors going to Africa and back, and he had just got off the boat and was wondering what it was like outside, when who should come knocking at the door but Eeyore.

"Hallo, Eeyore," said Christopher Robin, as he opened the door and came out. "How are *you*?"

"It's snowing still," said Eeyore gloomily.

"So it is."

"*And* freezing."

"Is it?"

"Yes," said Eeyore. "However," he said, brightening up a little, "we haven't had an earthquake lately."

"What's the matter, Eeyore?"

"Nothing, Christopher Robin. Nothing important. I suppose you haven't seen a house or whatnot anywhere about?"

"What sort of a house?"

"Just a house."

"Who lives there?"

"I do. At least I thought I did. But I suppose I don't. After all, we can't all have houses."

"But, Eeyore, I didn't know—I always thought—"

"I don't know how it is, Christopher Robin, but what with all this snow and one thing and another, not to mention icicles and such-like, it isn't so Hot in my field about three o'clock in the morning as some people think it is. It isn't Close, if you know what I mean—not so as to be uncomfortable. It isn't Stuffy. In fact, Christopher Robin," he went on in a loud whisper, "quite-between-ourselves-and-don't-tell-anybody, it's Cold."

"Oh, Eeyore!"

"And I said to myself: The others will be sorry if I'm getting myself all cold. They haven't got Brains, any of them, only grey fluff that's blown into their heads by mistake, and they don't Think, but if it goes on snowing for another six weeks or so, one of them will begin to say to himself: 'Eeyore can't

76

be so very much too Hot about three o'clock in the morning.' And then it will Get About. And they'll be Sorry.''

"Oh, Eeyore!" said Christopher Robin, feeling very sorry already.

"I don't mean you, Christopher Robin. You're different. So what it all comes to is that I built myself a house down by my little wood."

"Did you really? How exciting!"

"The really exciting part," said Eeyore in his most melancholy voice, "is that when I left it this morning it was there, and when I came back it wasn't. Not at all very natural, and it was only Eeyore's house. But still I just wondered."

Christopher Robin didn't stop to wonder. He was already back in *his* house, putting on his waterproof hat, his waterproof boots and his waterproof macintosh as fast as he could.

"We'll go and look for it at once," he called out to Eeyore.

"Sometimes," said Eeyore, "when people have quite finished taking a person's house, there are one or two bits which they don't want and are rather glad for the person to take back, if you know what I mean. So I thought if we just went—"

"Come on," said Christopher Robin, and off they hurried, and in a very little time they got to the corner of the field by the side of the pine-wood, where Eeyore's house wasn't any longer.

"There!" said Eeyore. "Not a stick of it left! Of course, I've still got all this snow to do what I like with. One mustn't complain."

But Christopher Robin wasn't listening to Eeyore, he was listening to something else.

"Can't you hear it?" he asked.

"What is it? Somebody laughing?"

"Listen."

They both listened . . . and they heard a deep gruff voice saying in a singing voice that the more it snowed the more it went on snowing and a small high voice tiddely-pomming in between.

"It's Pooh," said Christopher Robin excitedly. . . .

"Possibly," said Eeyore.

"*And* Piglet!" said Christopher Robin excitedly.

"Probably," said Eeyore. "What we *want* is a Trained Bloodhound."

The words of the song changed suddenly.

*"We've finished our HOUSE!"* sang the gruff voice.

*"Tiddely pom!"* sang the squeaky one.

*"It's a beautiful HOUSE . . ."*

*"Tiddely pom . . ."*

*"I wish it were MINE. . . ."*

*"Tiddely pom. . . ."*

"Pooh!" shouted Christopher Robin. . . .

The singers on the gate stopped suddenly.

"It's Christopher Robin!" said Pooh eagerly.

"He's round by the place where we got all those sticks from," said Piglet.

"Come on," said Pooh.

They climbed down their gate and hurried round the corner of the wood, Pooh making welcoming noises all the way.

"Why, here *is* Eeyore," said Pooh, when he had finished hugging Christopher Robin, and he nudged Piglet, and Piglet nudged him, and they thought to themselves what a lovely surprise they had got ready.

"Hallo, Eeyore."

"Same to you, Pooh Bear, and twice on Thursdays," said Eeyore gloomily.

Before Pooh could say: "Why Thursdays?" Christopher Robin began to explain the sad story of Eeyore's Lost House. And Pooh and Piglet listened, and their eyes seemed to get bigger and bigger.

"*Where* did you say it was?" asked Pooh.

"Just here," said Eeyore.

"Made of sticks?"

"Yes."

"Oh!" said Piglet.

"What?" said Eeyore.

"I just said 'Oh!'" said Piglet nervously. And so as to seem quite at ease he hummed Tiddely-pom once or twice in a what-shall-we-do-now kind of way.

"You're sure it *was* a house?" said Pooh. "I mean, you're sure the house was just here?"

"Of course I am," said Eeyore. And he

murmured to himself, "No brain at all some of them."

"Why, what's the matter, Pooh?" asked Christopher Robin.

"Well," said Pooh. . . . "The fact *is*," said Pooh . . . "Well, the fact *is*," said Pooh . . . "You see," said Pooh. . . . "It's like this," said Pooh, and something seemed to tell him that he wasn't explaining very well, and he nudged Piglet again.

"It's like this," said Piglet quickly. . . . "Only warmer," he added after deep thought.

"What's warmer?"

"The other side of the wood, where Eeyore's house is."

"*My* house?" said Eeyore. "My house was here."

"No," said Piglet firmly. "The other side of the wood."

"Because of being warmer," said Pooh.

"But I ought to *know* —"

"Come and look," said Piglet simply, and he led the way.

"There wouldn't be *two* houses," said Pooh. "Not so close together."

They came round the corner, and there was Eeyore's house, looking as comfy as anything.

"There you are," said Piglet.

"Inside as well as outside," said Pooh proudly.

Eeyore went inside . . . and came out again.

"It's a remarkable thing," he said. "It *is* my house, and I built it where I said I did, so the wind must have blown it here. And the wind blew it right over the wood, and blew it down here, and

here it is as good as ever. In fact, better in places."

"Much better," said Pooh and Piglet together.

"It just shows what can be done by taking a little trouble," said Eeyore. "Do you see, Pooh? Do you see, Piglet? Brains first and then Hard Work. Look at it! *That's* the way to build a house," said Eeyore proudly.

So they left him in it; and Christopher Robin went back to lunch with his friends Pooh and Piglet, and on the way they told him of the Awful Mistake they had made. And when he had finished laughing, they all sang the Outdoor Song for

Snowy Weather the rest of the way home, Piglet, who was still not quite sure of his voice, putting in the tiddely-poms again.

"And I know it *seems* easy," said Piglet to himself, "but it isn't *every one* who could do it."

## A Reader Says

*Pooh and Piglet wanted to do something nice, but I think Eeyore will miss his old house.*

How did you feel about the story?

# About the Author

## A. A. Milne

A. A. Milne lived in London, England. As a young man, he wrote funny plays. He also wrote funny articles for a magazine.

When his son, Christopher Robin, was young, Milne began to write poems for him. The poems were well liked and are classics today. They were put into two books, *When We Were Very Young* and *Now We Are Six*.

Mr. Milne also decided to write stories about his son's stuffed animals. They became famous. For 40 years, children have grown up reading about Pooh, Piglet, Kanga, Roo, and Eeyore. The story of these animals is told in *Winnie-the-Pooh* and *The House at Pooh Corner*. In these books, Christopher Robin and his stuffed animals have adventures in a forest called the Hundred Acre Wood.

Many parents love to make up stories for their children. It is interesting that Mr. Milne's greatest work as a writer was done when he wrote for his own son.

# More Books About Builders

**Harlequin and the Gift of Many Colors**
*by Remy Charlip*
When Harlequin can't afford a costume for the carnival, his friends get together to make him the most beautiful costume of all.

**A Chair for My Mother**
*by Vera B. Williams*
After the family home burns down, the children work together to get their mother a nice, soft chair to replace the one she lost. A heartwarming story of rebuilding after disaster.

**The Lorax**
*by Dr. Suess*
Not all things that people build are necessarily good. When a new building causes problems in the Lorax's land, he does everything he can to put a stop to it.

**Skyscraper Going Up!**
*by Vicki Cobb*
One of the hardest things to build is a skyscraper. This book will tell you all about the work that must be done to make one of these special buildings.

# MAKING ALL THE
# CONNECTIONS

## Speaking and Listening

The stories you read in this part of the book all told about builders. You read about Mr. Plumbean and his neighbors, who changed the street they live on. You read about Pooh and Piglet, who decided to build a house for Eeyore. You read about a family who worked together to make a quilt. You also read about how muscles help us to be builders.

The characters in the stories you read all built different things. How are the characters alike? How are they different? Discuss the stories you read with your classmates. You may want to look at your Reader's Log. Use the following questions to guide your discussion.

1. What did the characters in each story build or make?

2. Think about the things you have built. How are they like the things you read about in this part of the book? How are they different?

3. People can build houses, friendships, or new kinds of things. What other kinds of things can people build? Discuss all the kinds of things people build. Add ideas of you own. Make a list of the different things people can build.

# Building a Readers' Theater

## Planning

What is a readers' theater? In a readers' theater there are no stage, no costumes, and no scenery. Actors do not memorize their lines and act them out on stage. In a readers' theater, actors sit and read their lines aloud to an audience. Think about the stories you read in this unit. Think about how the stories would be as a readers' theater.

Look at the stories listed below. Think about the number of characters in each story. Will a narrator be needed to read those parts of the story that are not dialogue?

*Sails in the Sky*
*The Big Orange Splot*
*Do You Have the Time, Lydia?*
*The Patchwork Quilt*
*In Which A House Is Built at Pooh Corner*

Decide with your classmates how many actors will be needed for each story. Make a list like the one below for each story. Then decide which story each of you will be in. Together you will build your own readers' theater.

Actors needed for *The Patchwork Quilt*

| | | |
|---|---|---|
| Narrator | Papa | Ted |
| Tanya | Mama | Jim |
| Grandma | | |

**MAKING ALL THE CONNECTIONS**

## Working Together

Meet with the other students who will be in the story you have chosen. Decide which part each of you will take. Read through the story together. Find the lines that each character has. Find the parts where no character is speaking. Those are the parts that will be read by the narrator.

Now read through your part a number of times. Practice reading your lines with feeling. Think about how your character would say each line. Are any parts of the story funny? What can you do to add humor to those parts?

When you are comfortable with your lines, read them to a partner. Work with your partner to make sure you are speaking clearly and expressing yourself correctly. Listen to your partner's suggestions.

When everyone has had a chance to practice, rehearse the story together as a group. Practice until each character can say his or her lines in a natural way. Make sure your story flows smoothly and easily.

## Presenting

Now you and your group are ready to present your story as a readers' theater. You can share your stories in the following ways:

**Theater in the Classroom**   Present your story as a readers' theater to your class or another class in your school. Listen to other groups. How is the way they do the story different from yours? What do the other groups do to make the story more interesting or funny? What did you learn from the other groups that would make the reading of your story better?

**Put It on Tape**   Using a tape recorder, record your story with your group. Share the tape with another class. You may also want to set up the tape recorder in the school library, where other students might enjoy listening to your readers' theater.

# PART TWO

# Dreamers

Hold fast to dreams
For if dreams die
Life is a broken-winged bird
That cannot fly.

Hold fast to dreams
For when dreams go
Life is a barren field
Frozen with snow.

*Dreams*
by Langston Hughes

◆

Dreams are wishes and hopes that live in our hearts. The people you'll meet in the stories that follow all have special dreams that mean a lot to them. As you read, think: What dreams do you have that you hope come true?

# Exploring Words About Dreamers

## Starting with What You Know

Is a dreamer always a person who is sleeping? What other kinds of dreamers can you think of? The words in the box below tell about dreamers. Use these words and words of your own to answer the questions after the box.

| plan | creative | search |
|------|----------|--------|
| work | discover | curious |
| receive | explore | practice |

Many dreamers want to receive something. What else might a dreamer want to do? Dreamers are often curious. How else might you describe a dreamer? Dreamers often search to find their dream. What else might a dreamer do to find his or her dream?

## Building a Word Map

The word map shows how some of the words in the box above go together. Think about words you can add to the map. Use words from the box and other words of your own.

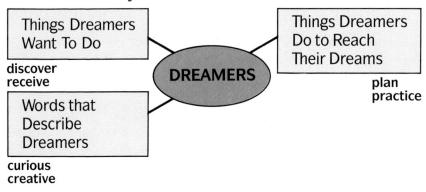

Things Dreamers Want To Do
discover
receive

Words that Describe Dreamers
curious
creative

DREAMERS

Things Dreamers Do to Reach Their Dreams
plan
practice

## Finishing a Story

Look at the story below. The story tells about a boy with a dream and how he makes his dream come true. Some words are missing. Think of words you would use to finish the story. Use the words from the box and word map in this lesson for ideas. Complete the story.

Tony had a dream. He wanted to _____ the way the school yard looked. He thought flowers would make it prettier.

Tony was a _____ boy. He had a _____. He asked other students for help.

On Saturday, the students went to the school yard. They had to _____ flower beds. They _____ the flowers. They all worked very _____. Now the school yard looks _____.

Share your story with your classmates. How were the stories different? What words did your classmates use?

## As You Read

In this part of the book, you will read about dreamers and the dreams they had. Keeping a Reader's Log will help you remember important thoughts, ideas, and words. As you read, make notes in your log. You could begin your Reader's Log with the word map. Add new words to the map as you find them.

In this story, a young girl sets out on an amazing journey. Is it real, or just a dream?

# The Girl Who Wished for a Star

## by Sarah Goldish

Once there was a girl who loved to look at the stars. Each night, she would sit up in bed and gaze out her window at the blanket of stars that covered the sky.

One night the girl made a wish, and this is what she said, "Oh, how they twinkle. Oh, how they shine. Oh, if just one little star could be mine!"

No sooner had she made her wish, than a small gray bird landed on the window sill.

"Hello," the bird said. "Why do you look so sad?"

"Oh, bird," the girl replied, "how lucky you are. For you can fly up, up to the stars. I would so like to have a star for myself. But I cannot fly."

"You may not fly," the bird said, "but you can still have your wish."

"I can?" the girl asked. "But how?"

"Just follow me," the bird said. "Walk to the place where I lead you. Walk to the place where I fly."

The girl got dressed quickly and went outside. The gray bird began to fly, and the girl followed. Soon they came to a long road.

"This is as far as I can take you," the bird said, and she flew away. For a moment all was quiet. Then the girl saw a silvery gray horse standing nearby.

"Good evening," the horse said. "How are you this grand, starry night?"

"Oh, horse," the girl said, "I am trying to get a star from the sky. But I don't know how."

"Maybe I can help you," the horse said. "Here, climb on my back, and I will take you to the stars."

Happily, the girl climbed up on the horse, and off they went. The horse ran and ran and ran, until he'd come to a place where the land ended. In front of them lay the wide waters of the ocean.

Up in the sky, the girl could see the twinkling stars bigger and brighter than they had ever looked before.

"This is as far as I can take you," the horse said. "You must find another way to go from here."

The girl climbed down from the horse, and he ran away.

**95**

As the girl looked out over the water, she saw a dolphin that shone as silver as starlight.

"Hello, little girl," the dolphin said. "You look so sad. Is there a way I can help you?"

"Oh, dolphin," the girl said sadly, "I want so much to have a twinkling star for myself. But I do not know how to get one."

"I think I can help you," the dolphin said. "Get on my back, and we will go."

The girl sat on the dolphin's back, and the dolphin swam far, far across the ocean until the girl could see a rainbow shimmering above the water. At last they came to a place where one end of the rainbow dipped into the water.

"This is as far as I can take you," the dolphin said. "Now you must climb up the rainbow. When you reach the top, you will be able to pluck a star from the sky. When you get to the top, grab one star in your hand and hold it tight."

Slowly, the girl began to climb up the long rainbow. The sky seemed to get brighter and brighter as she moved higher and higher, and the stars became closer and closer.

At last the girl reached the very top of the rainbow. There were the bright, twinkling stars—right in front of her eyes. Each star glowed like a fancy jewel. The girl was filled with joy.

The girl reached out to take a star. She leaned over and held out her right hand. Just as her hand touched the star, the rainbow seemed to melt away. The girl felt herself falling, falling, down through the sky and the black night.

She was falling so fast that she had no time to feel afraid.

For a little while, all the girl saw was darkness. Then she began to see the pale light of early morning. She looked around amazed to find herself back in her own bed in her own house.

"Alas," the girl sighed. "My wonderful trip to the stars was only a dream! I did not really get my wish after all."

Then the girl looked down at her closed hand. Slowly, she opened her hand and saw specks of twinkling silver dust—stardust!

## Thinking About the Theme

**1.** What makes you wonder if the girl's journey was real or just a dream?

**2.** Imagine you could dream up a place and travel there. What would it be like? What is there?

# Making Predictions

## Starting with What You Know

What will happen to the flower?

## Thinking About Predictions

When you read, you can sometimes imagine what will happen next. When you imagine what will happen next, you are making a **prediction**. One way to **predict** what will happen next is to think about what you already know. Another way is to look for clues that tell you what might happen. Read the paragraph. Choose the sentence on the next page that tells what will happen next.

Joseph planted flower seeds in his garden. The seeds began to grow, but Joseph forgot about them. The weather grew hotter and the ground became drier.

**a.** The flowers will grow well.

**b.** The flowers will die unless they get water.

You probably imagined that the flowers would die unless they were watered. You already know that plants need water, and the paragraph gave you clues that there was not enough water.

## Practice

Read the paragraph. Imagine what will happen next. Tell why you think as you do.

> Mrs. Quigley was a rich woman who loved to swim. When summer came, she had her driver take her to the city swimming pool every day. But the pool was always crowded. Mrs. Quigley didn't like it. One night she had a dream. She dreamed of a pool of her very own. The next day, she went outside to look at her big yard.

## As You Read

Making predictions helps you understand what happens in a story. Ask yourself these questions:

◆ What do I already know about what is happening?

◆ What clues does the story give me?

◆ What can I imagine that makes sense?

Apply what you know about making predictions as you read the two selections that follow. Use the side notes to help you.

Do we really want everything we dream of? In this Greek myth, King Midas finds out that a dream come true isn't always for the best.

# The Golden Touch

based on a retelling by Nathaniel Hawthorne

Once upon a time there lived a very wealthy king named Midas.

King Midas was fonder of gold than of anything else in the world. If he loved anything better, it was his daughter, Marygold. But the more he adored his daughter, the more he wanted to save her all the riches he could.

As days passed, Midas got to be so greedy that he could hardly stand to see or touch anything that was not gold. He spent almost every day in a dark room in the basement of his palace where he kept his riches. After carefully locking the door, he would gather gold coins and bring them into the one bright and narrow sunbeam that fell from the window. The only reason he loved that sunbeam was that his treasure wouldn't shine except for its aid.

King Midas has a problem. Think about what might happen.

Midas was in his treasure room one day when a shadow fell over the heaps of gold. King Midas quickly looked up, and saw a strange young man standing in the sunbeam.

"You are wealthy, King Midas," the stranger said. "No other room on earth contains as much gold and riches as you have in this room."

"I have done rather well," answered Midas, "but I could always use more."

This clue tells you what Midas wants.

"If you're not satisfied, what would satisfy you?" asked the stranger.

Midas thought about it for a moment. "I wish that everything I touch would change to gold!" King Midas exclaimed.

"The Golden Touch!" the stranger said. "That's a grand idea, but are you absolutely sure that this will satisfy you?"

The stranger asks Midas to think carefully. This might be a clue to what happens next.

"How could it fail?" said Midas.

"As you wish, then," replied the stranger. "Tomorrow, at sunrise, you will find yourself gifted with the Golden Touch."

The next morning, when the earliest sunbeam shone through the window onto his bedspread, King Midas looked closely and found that his bedspread had been changed into a fine gold cloth. The Golden Touch had come!

Midas leaped out of bed and ran about the room touching everything. He quickly put on his clothes and was delighted to see himself in a fancy robe of gold cloth.

He went downstairs, lifted the door latch (brass only a moment ago, but golden when he touched it), and went into his favorite rose garden. How he adored the delicate roses!

But Midas knew a way to make the roses far more valuable than they had ever been before. He went from bush to bush and touched each flower and changed it to gold. Rather pleased with his efforts, he went back inside.

Before long he heard Marygold sobbing, and he was upset, because Marygold was a happy girl.

Predict what will happen next.

"What is the matter with you this sunny morning?" asked Midas.

Marygold held out one of the roses that Midas had changed to gold.

"Beautiful!" exclaimed her father. "And why does this golden rose make you weep?"

"It is not beautiful but the ugliest flower that ever grew! As soon as I was dressed, I ran into the garden to gather some roses for you because I know they are your favorite flowers. But all the beautiful roses, that smelled so sweet and had so many delightful colors, are yellow and no longer have any smell! What is the matter with them?"

"My dear little girl, don't cry about it!" said Midas, who was ashamed to say that he himself had turned all the roses to gold. "Don't you see that a golden rose, which will last hundreds of years, is much more valuable than one that would wither in a day?"

"I don't care for such roses," cried Marygold, tossing it away, "that have no smell, and are so hard they prick my nose!"

King Midas felt so sorry for Marygold that he reached over to quiet her, and, without thinking, gave her a kiss.

"My dear, dear Marygold!" he cried.

But Marygold couldn't answer.

What had he done? The moment the lips of Midas touched Marygold's forehead, a change had occurred, and her sweet, rosy face and beautiful brown hair had turned yellow. Because of his love of wealth, little Marygold was no longer a child, but a golden statue.

It was a favorite saying of Midas's that his daughter, Marygold, was worth her weight in gold. But now, when it was too late, he felt how much more valuable she was to him than all the riches on earth.

Midas couldn't do anything except wring his hands, and wish that he owned nothing in the world if the loss of all his wealth might bring back his Marygold.

Think about whether or not this is what you predicted would happen.

Think about what Midas might do to bring back Marygold.

He suddenly saw a stranger standing in the door. Midas bent down his head quietly, for he knew it was the same young man who had appeared to him and given him the Golden Touch.

"Why are you so upset?" inquired the man.

"I've found out that gold is not everything," answered Midas, "and I've lost all that my heart really cared for."

"Ah! So you've made a discovery since yesterday!" said the stranger. "Which of these two do you think is really worth the most—the gift of the Golden Touch or your Marygold?"

"Oh, my child!" cried Midas.

"You are wiser than you were, King Midas," said the stranger. "Go, then, and dive into the river below your garden, and take a vase of the water and sprinkle it over the statue of Marygold and whatever else you want to change back again from gold."

King Midas bowed low, and when he lifted his head, the stranger had vanished.

Midas lost no time in snatching up a large vase and running to the riverside, where he dove headfirst into the river.

He dipped the vase into the water and quickly ran back to the palace. The first thing he did was sprinkle the water by handfuls over the golden statue of little Marygold.

Midas has learned a lesson. Predict how he will act from now on.

No sooner did it fall on her than the rosy color came back to her face, and she was surprised to find herself dripping wet and her father still tossing more water over her!

Next he led little Marygold into the garden, where he sprinkled water over the roses. They once again bloomed in beautiful colors and smelled as sweet as ever.

From then on, King Midas hated all gold except for his Marygold's golden hair which remained that color to remind him of the Golden Touch.

## A Reader Says

*King Midas should've known that not everything should be gold. I'm glad I don't have the Golden Touch!*

How did you feel about the story?

# After You Read

## Thinking About What You Read

1. King Midas was a very rich man. Why do you think he wanted even more gold?

2. Why do you think that the stranger granted King Midas's wish?

3. Which do you think is more beautiful, a golden rose or one that nature made? Why do you think so?

4. What lesson do you think King Midas learned about the "golden touch"?

## Thinking About How You Read

How did knowing that everything Midas touched would turn to gold help you guess what would happen near the end of the story?

## Sharing and Listening

What dream do you have that you would like to come true? Talk about your dream with the class. Listen to your classmates as they tell about their dreams.

## Writing

Write two sentences that tell why you think King Midas liked gold so much.

It takes hard work and practice to make some dreams come true. Marsha longs to be a figure-skating champion. Can she get her wish just by dreaming?

# The Skates of Uncle Richard

## by Carol Fenner

*Nine-year-old Marsha dreamed about a beautiful, tall, slender ice-skating champion who could leap high into the air and spin very fast. Marsha, in real life, had been watching the skaters on T.V. since she was six. She had never skated on real skates, but often she would pretend to skate when she was alone. But pretend skating was not the same as dreaming of being the beautiful ice-skating champion.*

The days grew shorter and shorter. Winter was really on its way, and thoughts of her birthday came into Marsha's dreaming head. She began to hint to her mother that she sure would like ice skates for her birthday this year.

"When you can watch where you're walking, and when you can wipe the silverware without dropping it," her mother said, "maybe then you can handle ice skates."

Marsha had never thought to watch where she walked or to keep hold of the silverware, because she had more exciting things on her mind. But even if she seriously tried hard to be more alert, Marsha didn't think she would ever get ice skates for her birthday.

Marsha worried about what would happen to the beautiful skater in her head if the real Marsha ever got real ice skates on her real feet. Her dream skating, her leaps and spins, might not come true at all.

After a while, whenever Marsha brought up the subject of ice skates, her mother would look sort of thoughtful. Marsha's hopes rose, but her worry about losing the dream skater who lived in her head rose, too.

Now her birthday was here. Marsha's eyes flew over the gifts to a large box covered with red tissue. It had silver stars pasted into the shape of a big starry M. Marsha's heart crowded into her throat.

She couldn't bring herself to open the red box right away. First she unwrapped a new dress with a lace collar and two new books. But her mind was on the box covered with red tissue. She grew first hot, then cold, from excitement.

She opened a paint set. Her older brother, Leonard, gave her a flashlight. Finally the box covered with red tissue was the only one left to open.

She tore at the tissue, careful not to rip into the big *M*. The box inside looked like the one her last year's winter boots had come in. When she opened it up, there inside the whispering tissue bulged the ugliest ice skates she had ever seen.

For a while, Marsha just sat staring at the skates. Then she took them out of the box. They were old-fashioned hockey skates, not in the least the kind of skates a figure skater would wear.

"They were your uncle Richard's skates," said her mother, "when he was seven. He was about your size then. He kept them up real nice so they're almost good as new."

Marsha kept her eyes on the skates. Uncle Richard was old now, at least thirty. She could feel tears pushing to get out from behind her eyes.

"Your uncle Richard is a fine skater," her mother continued. "He learned how to skate on those skates. They'll be a good start for you, Marsha, till we see how serious you are about skating."

Marsha sat on the floor with the ugly skates in her lap. "I remembered packing them away in the attic years ago," her mother was saying. "Richard'll be pleased to know they're being used." She added tartly, "If he ever stops by long enough to talk."

But Marsha was feeling the beautiful skating champion inside her head disappear. Her dream had left her and the ugliest skates in the world lay in her lap.

One Saturday, several weeks after her birthday, Leonard agreed to take Marsha skating at the lagoon. Marsha had stuffed the skates under her bed. She took them out. They fit, but her ankles wobbled. Maybe it would be different on the ice.

But it wasn't different. She kept falling down. It wasn't fun and her ankles began to ache. Finally, Leonard pulled her across the ice to a bench and went to skate with his friends.

Marsha sat on the bench, sad and alone. She wanted to go home, but she didn't know how she would ever get back across the frozen lagoon.

Suddenly, a man skated up and stopped in front of her, smiling. She saw he was leaning forward saying something, and she recognized her uncle Richard. He was saying, "Marsha, why are you looking so sad?"

Marsha didn't know how to tell him, so she changed the subject. "Momma's mad at you again," she said shyly, "because you haven't been by."

"Your momma is always mad at me," said Uncle Richard. "I was out of town," he added absently. Marsha saw he was studying her skates. "Why don't you lace up your skates properly?" he asked. As he bent way over and touched them thoughtfully, Marsha could see he was puzzled.

"They were your first skates when you were seven," she explained in a low voice. Uncle Richard knelt down in front of her and took one of her feet in both of his hands. "Yeah," he whispered, "they sure are." He looked up at her with happiness growing in his face. "Those good old skates." He laughed and then he began to undo the laces. "First off, Marsha, you've got to have your skates laced properly."

Then he said, "Here's something else to practice." He pushed forward into one foot and trailed the other behind lightly without touching the ice. "Just bend your knee and lean into it," he said, "nice and easy."

"Now you practice that for a while." Marsha nodded and Uncle Richard skated off. She watched to see if he really could skate as well as her mother said.

Marsha saw him reach into his pocket and pull out a tiny radio. He held it close to his head and began to skate to songs no one else could hear. Marsha noticed he glided a long time on one foot before he shifted his weight to the other one.

His speed quickened, then he circled into a spin that blurred his entire outline.

"Oh," breathed Marsha, "he is really fine."

Suddenly he swooped and leapt into a single axle. He circled to a halt and began to skate backward, disappearing around a bend in the little island.

Alone in the middle of the ice, Marsha felt her ankles begin to wobble with worry. She tried resting them the way Uncle Richard had taught her and they stopped wobbling. "But I can't stand here forever," she thought. She tested herself, lifting first one foot and then the other.

Then she took a deep breath, bent her knee, and pushed off into her right foot the way Uncle Richard had done. She glided a little, her body balanced over her skating foot. Then she shifted and pushed into her left foot and glided a shaky distance. It worked! Push, glide . . . push, glide. It was fun!

Suddenly she realized she was at the other end of the lagoon. "My, my," said a voice behind her. "I thought I left you down at the other end." It was Uncle Richard. "How did you get here?" he asked.

"I push-push-glided till I got here," said Marsha.

"You're one surprising young lady," said Uncle Richard. "You sure learn fast." He bent down and looked seriously into her face.

Marsha felt, in that moment, that Uncle Richard could see inside her heart better than anyone. The beautiful champion figure skater of her dreams floated briefly into her mind, but Marsha didn't have time for her now.

Uncle Richard laced the skates very tightly and evenly across her foot and ankle.

Then he stood her up and began to pull her slowly and evenly across the ice. "Bend your knees, not your middle," he told her. When she did so, she was surprised at how easily she could balance.

After they had gone a short distance, Uncle Richard said, "You do that real easy, so I want to show you some things to practice here while I get some skating done." First he showed Marsha how to rest her ankles whenever they got tired. "Stand quietly. Breathe easy. Let your feet go soft."

"I want to learn how to skate like you skate," she said. Uncle Richard touched her cheek softly with his fingertips. He looked very thoughtful for a minute, then he said quietly, "Okay, we'll work on it. But you'll have to set your mind to it."

Marsha nodded again. She understood.

Uncle Richard suddenly laughed out loud. "We'll surprise your momma," he said. "Next week we'll practice some more. I'll talk to your momma and maybe she won't be mad at me."

Marsha beamed at him.

"They are a good old pair of skates," he said. "Oil the runners, you hear?" Marsha nodded.

Uncle Richard pushed off. Marsha followed, and glided away on the skates of Uncle Richard, taller and taller, never once falling down.

## A Reader Says

*I bet if Marsha practices a lot, her Mom will get her new skates for her next birthday.*

How did you feel about the story?

# After You Read

## Thinking About What You Read

**1.** Marsha wants skates very badly. Yet, she is afraid that if she gets skates her dream skater will disappear. Why do you think she feels the way she does?

**2.** Do you think it was a good idea to give Uncle Richard's skates to Marsha? Why or why not?

**3.** Why do you think that seeing Marsha wearing his old skates makes Uncle Richard happy?

**4.** Why do you think Marsha felt that Uncle Richard could see into her heart better than anyone else?

## Thinking About How You Read

How did knowing what Marsha really wanted help you guess how she would feel when she opened her birthday present?

## Sharing and Listening

Do you think that Marsha will work hard at her skating? Talk about why you think so or why you think not. Listen as the others in your class tell what they think.

## Writing

Make believe that you are Marsha. Write two or three sentences in your diary about your dream of becoming a champion skater.

# Understanding Science Selections

### Starting with What You Know

You know that plants and fish are living things. They need water and food. You know these things because you know something about science. What do you know about some other living things?

### Thinking About Science

In **science,** you learn about real things in the world. A science selection is not made up the way some stories are. Science selections are **nonfiction.** Nonfiction selections have the following:

Topic: This is what the story is about, such as birds or weather.

Main Ideas: These are the important things you learn as you read.

Headings: These are groups of words in dark print. They tell you what you will read about in each part of the story.

Pictures: These give you more information about the topic.

## Before You Read

Look at the title of the selection. It will give you the topic. Look at the pictures and the headings. Think about what you already know about the topic. Think of a question about the topic.

## As You Read

Read slowly. Science selections are interesting, but sometimes they are hard to read. Stop after every page, and think about what you have read. Ask yourself these questions. The questions with blue diamonds are for any kind of nonfiction. The questions with red diamonds are for science selections.

Topic: ◆ What is the selection about?

◆ What do I already know about this science topic?

Main Ideas: ◆ What are the important ideas?

◆ What new information and facts am I learning about this topic?

Headings: ◆ What will I find out in this part of the selection?

Pictures: ◆ What do they show about the topic?

Apply what you know about understanding science selections as you read the two science selections that follow. Use the side notes to help you.

**Maybe you remember a dream you had last night. This article will explain why you dream and the many things dreams can do.**

# Everything Begins with a Dream

by Donna Disch

The article begins by telling you what dreams are.

Each night when we go to sleep we see stories from our life. No matter what the story is about, while we are dreaming, it seems very real. Often we dream about feelings and things that have happened to us during the day or long ago. Other times, the dream is a wild story about places and people we've never seen before.

## Everyone Dreams

Notice the heading. Now you know what the next part will be about.

Every person on Earth dreams. Even animals and birds dream. Perhaps you have noticed a sleeping dog whimpering or pawing the air. Like us he is watching a story about himself. Perhaps he's burying a bone, or pawing a door he wants to open. He too, for the moment, believes the dream is real.

How do we know that all people and animals dream? For many years, scientists have studied sleepers. They noticed that their eyes moved rapidly back and forth beneath their eyelids. It looked as though they were watching a tennis ball being batted from court to court. Scientists wondered what this meant. They discovered that every time they awakened a sleeper whose eyes were moving, the sleeper always had a dream to tell.

The article tells you what scientists have learned.

**129**

The first dream happens about an hour after we fall asleep and lasts about ten minutes. We sleep for the next hour and then we dream again. Throughout the night, we dream four or five times. The last dream of the night is the longest. It lasts for about half an hour. It is this dream that we often remember when we wake up.

**Dreams Are Important to Health**

Think about what might happen if our bodies did not rest every night.

Even if we don't always remember our dreams, it is important to our health that we have them. Our bodies must rest every night. Our brains that think and learn all day long must also rest. Dreaming allows our brains to relax and get ready for the following day. When scientists have awakened sleepers each time they began to dream, the sleepers became very sad, worried, and tired. The next day they could not think clearly, learn new things, or remember things they had already learned.

**Dreaming Long Ago**

Today's scientists are not the first people to be interested in dreams. For thousands of years, people have tried to understand and use their dreams. The ancient Egyptians, Greeks, and Romans were as interested in dreams as we are today. They believed that dreams could tell the future. They wrote about their dreams in books and built beautiful temples and houses where people could dream happy and helpful dreams.

For thousands of years dreams have helped people in many ways. Great leaders have dreamed of how to win a battle before fighting it. Mathematicians have solved difficult problems while dreaming. Scientists have made important discoveries in their dreams. Song writers and authors have often said that they got the idea for a song or a story in a dream. How can this happen? Some scientists think that difficult problems are easier to solve when the mind is relaxed. When we sleep, our minds are resting. That is why the answer to a problem we've been struggling with might appear in a dream.

Dreams help people in important ways. Imagine how a dream might help someone.

Notice how daydreams are different from night dreams.

### Daydreams

But our dreams do not end with the night. Daydreams happen anytime we let our minds wander away from what is really happening. Like night dreams, we see a story in our minds, but with daydreams we decide exactly what happens, and we are never fooled into thinking it's real. We daydream most often when we are alone, or just before we fall asleep. But daydreams or waking dreams can happen anytime.

### "Stream of Thought"

When scientists talk about daydreams, they say that we drift in a "stream of thought." Imagine yourself floating down a stream filled not with water, but with ideas and pictures. Imagine that the stream pushes you along, as you swim and play with the ideas and pictures that you like most. Daydreams allow us to play with such subjects as what we might like to see, where we might like to go, or what we might like to be someday. In a daydream, we can spend a hot afternoon in an igloo, or dive with dolphins in the warm South Seas. Daydreams allow us to imagine whatever we like.

## How Daydreams Help Us

Daydreams can also help us solve problems.
When we are alone, we can talk to ourselves.
Before we decide what's best to do, we can ask
ourselves things like "what would happen if . . .?"
or "would it be a good idea to . . .?" Then we can
imagine what might happen. This way we can see
difficulties that might occur and how to avoid
them.

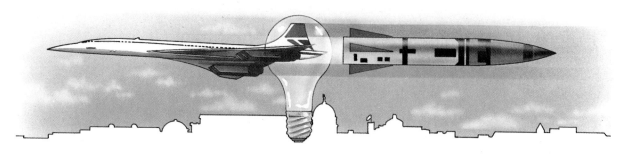

Inventors and great thinkers asked themselves such things and came up with wonderful ideas. Just about any great invention you can think of was first imagined in a daydream. The electric light bulb, the airplane, the rocket, even some cities, like Washington, D.C., were all first a picture in someone's mind. Even more than night dreams, daydreams have brought about many great inventions and important scientific discoveries.

Think of inventions you've daydreamed about.

### Scientists Continue to Study Dreams

Scientists who study dreams are learning more and more all the time. But there is still a lot about dreaming we don't know. No one knows exactly why we dream what we do or how dreams happen. We don't know what makes dreams seem so real. Most important, we don't completely understand what dreams are for. We do know, however, that we use dreams to relax and to help solve problems. We know that both day and night dreams are normal and lead to healthier and happier lives.

Think about what else scientists might find as they study dreams.

### A Reader Says

*I'd like to write a story about a dream I once had.*

How did you feel about the article?

# After You Read

## Thinking About What You Read

**1.** Why do you think that people's eyes move back and forth when they dream?

**2.** Long ago, people built beautiful houses where they could dream happy dreams. Do you think that a beautiful place can help make beautiful dreams? Why or why not?

**3.** How are daydreams and night dreams alike? How are they different?

**4.** What do you think life would be like if people did not dream?

## Thinking About How You Read

How did knowing about the parts of a science article help you ask questions as you read?

## Sharing and Listening

Why do you think that it is important for scientists to study about dreams? Talk about your ideas with the class. Listen to others as they tell their ideas.

## Writing

Write a few sentences telling about a funny dream you once had at night. If you cannot remember one, tell about a funny dream you would like to have.

# By Myself

When I'm by myself
And I close my eyes
I'm a twin
I'm a dimple in a chin
I'm a room full of toys
I'm a squeaky noise
I'm a gospel song
I'm a gong
I'm a leaf turning red
I'm a loaf of brown bread
I'm a whatever I want to be
An anything I care to be
And when I open my eyes
What I care to be
Is me

Eloise Greenfield

Being a scientist is more than looking at facts. A good scientist, like Galileo, needs to have imagination, too. This article tells how he dreamed of trying things no one had thought of before.

# Galileo

## by Juan Gonzalez

What does it take to be a scientist? Studying in school is surely important. But more than that, it takes curiosity. You have to be interested in what is going on in nature. You have to wonder why things happen the way they do. Good scientists often use their imaginations to look at everyday things in a completely new way. That is the main reason they get ideas that no one ever had before.

A man named Galileo was one of the greatest scientists ever for this reason. All his life, he wanted to find out how things worked. His imagination and curiosity made it easier for him to learn more about nature than people had ever known before.

139

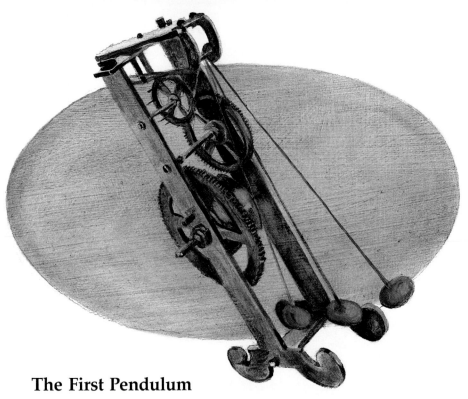

## The First Pendulum

Galileo made his first important discovery when he was only 20 years old. He was watching a lamp that was attached by a long chain to the ceiling. A breeze had made the lamp swing back and forth. At first, each swing was wide. Later the swings became shorter. But it looked to Galileo as if each swing was taking the same amount of time. Galileo tried to time the swings. He used his own pulse to do this. He found that he was right. To make sure, Galileo hurried home and attached a weight to a string. He swung the weight again and again. Long or short, the swings all took the same time. Galileo had discovered something very important about a **pendulum**, or a weight hung at the end of a long cord. His discovery was later used to make better clocks. A pendulum could keep a clock going at the same rate all the time.

Galileo found out how pendulums move for several reasons. For years, thousands of people had passed by that swinging lamp. No one had noticed anything special about it. But Galileo took a good look. The lamp's movement made him wonder. Then, when he got an idea about how the lamp moved, he tested it out by measuring the time each swing took. Later on, he built a simple pendulum. He repeated his test over and over. That way he could be sure that pendulums acted like this all the time, not just once in a while. Testing an idea like this is called an **experiment**. Galileo was one of the first people to use experiments to test out ideas.

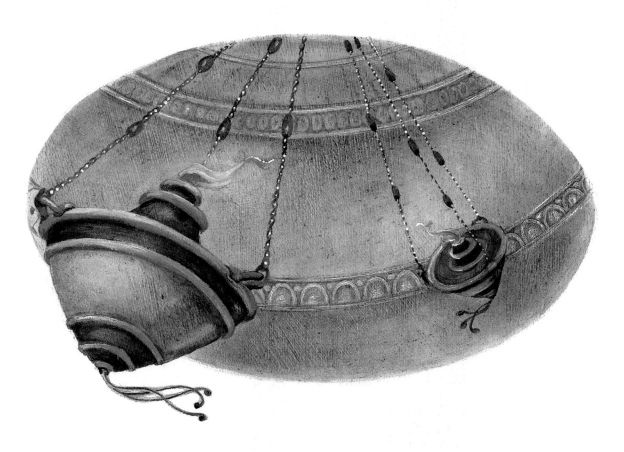

### The Law of Falling Bodies

In about 1590, Galileo tested out another idea. Until that time, people believed that heavier objects fell more quickly than light ones. It seems as if that would be true, doesn't it? But Galileo was not so sure. So he tried dropping two objects of unequal weights. Both objects landed on the ground at almost the same time. Many people disagreed with Galileo's idea. But Galileo could prove his idea by showing people his test again and again. People came to agree with Galileo. This law of nature that Galileo proved is called the law of falling bodies.

You can test the law of falling bodies for yourself. First get a paper clip or a coin. Then take a heavier object like a book, or even a sneaker. Next, hold both objects, one in each hand, high above your head. Finally, drop both objects at the same time. See whether they land at the same time.

## Galileo Studies the Planets

Galileo had now made two discoveries that would make him well-known from then on. But his curiosity was still great. He wanted to find out more about nature. The pendulum and the law of falling bodies had taught him a lot about how objects move. Now he began to wonder about how planets moved through space.

In 1609, Galileo heard of a new invention called a spyglass. The spyglass made faraway objects seem closer. The first spyglasses were not very powerful. They showed objects only about three times closer than they normally appeared. These spyglasses were the first **telescopes.** Galileo discovered how to build a better telescope. He used it to study the night sky. Again, he noticed important new facts.

At that time, nearly everyone believed that the moon was a smooth ball that shone with its own light as the sun did. They believed that the Milky Way was a band of light far up in the sky. Then Galileo started looking through his telescope, and these old ideas were proved wrong. First he got a good look at the moon: He saw that it was not a smooth glowing ball. Instead, it was full of mountains and deep pits. Besides, the light it gave off was reflected from the sun. Next, Galileo studied the Milky Way. He found that it was a thick cluster of stars, not a band of light.

## The Planets Circle the Sun

Galileo's work with his telescope made him wonder about another long-held idea. For hundreds of years, people had believed that the earth was the center of everything in space. They thought that the sun, moon, planets, and stars all moved around the earth, which was steady. In about 1540, a man named Copernicus wrote that this might not be so. He thought that all the planets including Earth circled the sun. Few people believed Copernicus. How could the earth possibly be moving through space? For one thing, it felt steady. For another, if it moved, it would soon leave the moon, its closest neighbor, behind. Copernicus had to be wrong.

Galileo didn't agree. Copernicus's map of the sky sounded right to him. But he had no firm proof. Then one night, he noticed several tiny points of light near the planet Jupiter. He studied these objects night after night through his telescope. They seemed to be traveling around Jupiter. They must be moons of Jupiter! Galileo was very excited. Everyone believed that all space bodies circled the earth. Yet here were four moons circling Jupiter. That meant that the planets themselves did not have to be circling Earth either. They could be traveling around the sun. Besides, Jupiter was known to be a moving body. Yet it did not leave its moons behind as it traveled through the sky. That meant that Earth wouldn't have to leave its moon behind if it moved. Here at last was proof that Copernicus could be right.

Galileo wrote about his findings in several books. At first, many people were upset about what he had written. They did not want Galileo's ideas to be heard. But Galileo had the last word. In time, other scientists found more proof that the earth moved around the sun. Today, few people remember the names of the people who tried to silence Galileo. But Galileo's name is remembered and respected by scientists everywhere.

## A Reader Says

*I would like to look through a telescope at the stars and planets the way Galileo did.*

How did you feel about the article?

# After You Read

## Thinking About What You Read

**1.** How do you think that curiosity helps a person become a good scientist?

**2.** Galileo tried his pendulum experiment over and over again. Why do you think that scientists try the same thing again and again and again?

**3.** Why do you think that Galileo's findings upset many people?

**4.** Which of Galileo's discoveries surprised you the most? Why?

## Thinking About How You Read

How did knowing about science articles help you find important facts about Galileo's work?

## Sharing and Listening

Do you have a favorite dream? Do you think Galileo had one? What do you think it was? Talk about your ideas with your classmates. Listen as they tell you their ideas.

## Writing

If you could meet Galileo, what questions would you like to ask him? Write two or three questions to ask Galileo. Tell why you want to know these things.

Sometimes it takes a long time to make dreams
come true. Ever since Miss Rumphius was a child,
she wanted to do three things. Read to see if she
can do everything she's planned.

# Miss Rumphius

◆

### by Barbara Cooney

The Lupine Lady lives in a small house
overlooking the sea. In between the rocks around
her house grow blue and purple and rose-colored
flowers. The Lupine Lady is little and old. But she
has not always been that way. I know. She is my
great-aunt, and she told me so.

Once upon a time she was a little girl named
Alice, who lived in a city by the sea. From the front
stoop she could see the wharves and the bristling
masts of tall ships. Many years ago her grandfather
had come to America on a large sailing ship.

Now he worked in the shop at the bottom of the house, making figureheads for the prows of ships, and carving Indians out of wood to put in front of cigar stores. For Alice's grandfather was an artist. He painted pictures, too, of sailing ships and places across the sea. When he was very busy, Alice helped him put in the skies.

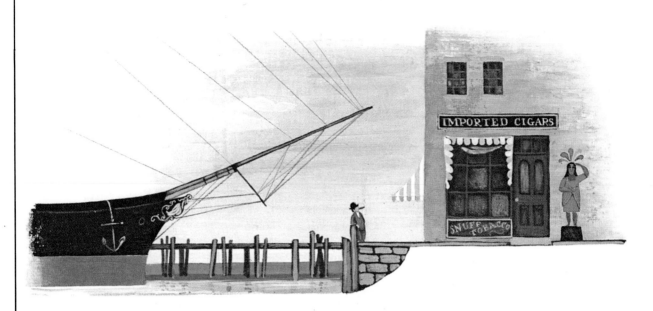

In the evening Alice sat on her grandfather's knee and listened to his stories of faraway places. When he had finished, Alice would say, "When I grow up, I too will go to faraway places, and when I grow old, I too will live beside the sea."

"That is all very well, little Alice," said her grandfather, "but there is a third thing you must do."

"What is that?" asked Alice.

"You must do something to make the world more beautiful," said her grandfather.

"All right," said Alice. But she did not know what that could be.

In the meantime Alice got up and washed her face and ate porridge for breakfast. She went to school and came home and did her homework.

And pretty soon she was grown up.

Then my Great-aunt Alice set out to do the three
things she had told her grandfather she was going
to do. She left home and went to live in another
city far from the sea and the salt air. There she
worked in a library, dusting books and keeping
them from getting mixed up, and helping people
find the ones they wanted. Some of the books told
her about faraway places.

People called her Miss Rumphius now.

Sometimes she went to the conservatory in the middle of the park. When she stepped inside on a wintry day, the warm moist air wrapped itself around her, and the sweet smell of jasmine filled her nose.

"This is almost like a tropical isle," said Miss Rumphius. "But not quite."

So Miss Rumphius went to a real tropical island, where people kept cockatoos and monkeys as pets. She walked on long beaches, picking up beautiful shells. One day she met the Bapa Raja, king of a fishing village.

"You must be tired," he said. "Come into my house and rest."

So Miss Rumphius went in and met the Bapa Raja's wife. The Bapa Raja himself fetched a green coconut and cut a slice off the top so that Miss Rumphius could drink the coconut water inside. Before she left, the Bapa Raja gave her a beautiful mother-of-pearl shell on which he had painted a bird of paradise and the words, "You will always remain in my heart."

"You will always remain in mine too," said Miss Rumphius.

My great-aunt Miss Alice Rumphius climbed tall
mountains where the snow never melted. She went
through jungles and across deserts. She saw lions
playing and kangaroos jumping. And everywhere
she made friends she would never forget. Finally
she came to the Land of the Lotus-Eaters, and
there, getting off a camel, she hurt her back.

"What a foolish thing to do," said Miss
Rumphius. "Well, I have certainly seen faraway
places. Maybe it is time to find my place by the
sea."

And it was, and she did.

CAFE DJERBA

**155**

From the porch of her new house Miss Rumphius watched the sun come up; she watched it cross the heavens and sparkle on the water; and she saw it set in glory in the evening. She started a little garden among the rocks that surrounded her house, and she planted a few flower seeds in the stony ground. Miss Rumphius was *almost* perfectly happy.

"But there is still one more thing I have to do," she said. "I have to do something to make the world more beautiful."

But what? "The world already is pretty nice," she thought, looking out over the ocean.

The next spring Miss Rumphius was not very well. Her back was bothering her again, and she had to stay in bed most of the time.

The flowers she had planted the summer before had come up and bloomed in spite of the stony ground. She could see them from her bedroom window, blue and purple and rose-colored.

"Lupines," said Miss Rumphius with satisfaction. "I have always loved lupines the best. I wish I could plant more seeds this summer so that I could have still more flowers next year."

But she was not able to.

After a hard winter spring came. Miss Rumphius was feeling much better. Now she could take walks again. One afternoon she started to go up and over the hill, where she had not been in a long time.

"I don't believe my eyes!" she cried when she got
to the top. For there on the other side of the hill
was a large patch of blue and purple and
rose-colored lupines!

"It was the wind," she said as she knelt in
delight. "It was the wind that brought the seeds
from my garden here! And the birds must have
helped!"

Then Miss Rumphius had a wonderful idea!

She hurried home and got out her seed catalogues. She sent off to the very best seed house for five bushels of lupine seed.

All that summer Miss Rumphius, her pockets full of seeds, wandered over fields and headlands, sowing lupines. She scattered seeds along the highways and down the country lanes. She flung handfuls of them around the schoolhouse and back of the church. She tossed them into hollows and along stone walls.

Her back didn't hurt her any more at all.

Now some people called her That Crazy Old Lady.

The next spring there were lupines everywhere. Fields and hillsides were covered with blue and purple and rose-colored flowers. They bloomed along the highways and down the lanes. Bright patches lay around the schoolhouse and back of the church. Down in the hollows and along the stone walls grew the beautiful flowers.

Miss Rumphius had done the third, the most difficult thing of all!

My Great-aunt Alice, Miss Rumphius, is very old now. Her hair is very white. Every year there are more and more lupines. Now they call her the Lupine Lady. Sometimes my friends stand with me outside her gate, curious to see the old, old lady who planted the fields of lupines. When she invites us in, they come slowly. They think she is the oldest woman in the world. Often she tells us stories of faraway places.

"When I grow up," I tell her, "I too will go to faraway places and come home to live by the sea."

"That is all very well, little Alice," says my aunt, "but there is a third thing you must do."

"What is that?" I ask.

"You must do something to make the world more beautiful."

"All right," I say.

But I do not know yet what that can be.

## A Reader Says

*I think Miss Rumphius helped the world by making all those friends.*

How did you feel about the story?

# About the Author

## Barbara Cooney

Barbara Cooney has drawn the pictures for a hundred books. She is well-known for her beautiful, colorful pictures that are filled with details. Ms. Cooney has also written stories for more than ten books for children.

Two of her books, *Chanticleer and the Fox* and *Ox-Cart Man*, won Caldecott Medals. Ms. Cooney also won the American Book Award for the story you read, *Miss Rumphius*.

Ms. Cooney was born in New York City. After she grew up, she served in the army, married, and had four children. She now lives in Maine and Massachusetts. She says that her four children inspire her to make books for children. If they like her books, Ms. Cooney says, she thinks others may like them too.

# More Books About Dreamers

**Daydreamers**

*by Eloise Greenfield*

Eloise Greenfield, the prize-winning poet who wrote "By Myself" and many other poems and books, here writes poems about many different kinds of dreamers.

**The Hundred Dresses**

*by Eleanor Estes*

When a poor girl can't wear beautiful dresses to school, she finds another way to make her dreams come true. Read this book to find out a wonderful answer to a difficult problem.

**Jane Goodall: Living Chimp Style**

*by Mary V. Fox*

Jane Goodall was a special scientist. She dreamed of proving that chimps were smarter than many scientists thought. In this book, you'll see what she found out when she went to live with some chimps.

**Sam, Bangs, and Moonshine**

*by Evaline Ness*

Sam is a girl whose imagination sometimes gets out of hand. She finds out the hard way that her habit of "moonshining" can cause serious trouble! Now what will she do about it?

# MAKING ALL THE
# CONNECTIONS

## Speaking and Listening

The stories in this part of the book told about dreams and dreamers. You read about a king who dreamed of filling his life with gold. You read about a girl who dreamed of becoming a champion ice skater. You read about Galileo, whose curiosity and dreams helped to change science. You read an article that told how dreams can help you. You also read about Miss Rumphius, who made many of her dreams come true.

Think about the characters you read about and the dreams they had. Discuss the selections with your classmates. You may want to look at your Reader's Log. Speak loudly and clearly when you give your thoughts. Listen carefully to the thoughts of others. Use these questions to help you.

1. The characters in the stories you read all had dreams. How were these dreams alike? How were they different?

2. How are your own dreams like the dreams of the characters you read about?

3. Discuss with your classmates what the characters in the stories did to make their dreams come true.

# Reading Something New in Social Studies

*Mary McLeod Bethune was a woman with a dream. As you read the next story, discover her dream and what she did to make it come true.*

When I was six years old, my mama and I went to deliver laundry to a white family. One of the girls showed me a book about Africa. I wanted to read that book, but there was no school I could go to. Slavery was over, but there were no schools for black people.

The next year, a school opened and I was allowed to go. I learned to read, and then I continued my education. I became a teacher, but there was more for me to do.

I moved to Florida. There were no schools for black children. I decided to start one. I found a big, old house. People came to help clean and fix it up. I found things at the city dump that I used to make desks. Five students came the first week. Soon there were twenty.

The school was always short of money, but I was able to find people ready to help. Soon the school outgrew the house. I worked hard to raise money for a bigger school. Over the years, the school grew to 1,300 students and 19 buildings. My dream of providing education for black youngsters has come true.

**MAKING ALL THE CONNECTIONS**

# Thinking About Dreamers ◆

The story you just read about Mary McLeod Bethune was like the stories you have read in this part of the book. It is a story about a dream. What did Mary McLeod Bethune do to make her dream come true? What is the final outcome? Ask yourself the same questions about the stories you have read. Then copy this chart and use what you have read to complete it. The answers for King Midas have been filled in for you.

| Dreamer: Outcome | Dream | How Dreams Come True |
|---|---|---|
| Mary McLeod Bethune: | | |
| Galileo: | | |
| Marsha: | | |
| King Midas: learned gold wasn't everything. | Lots of gold | Magic touch |

Look back at your chart. You can see that there are all kinds of dreams. Think about a dream that you have had. What did you do to make your dream come true? What happened when it did come true? You can write about your dream. Write your name on the chart under King Midas'. Then complete the rest of the chart. You can add more than one dream to your chart and decide which you want to write about later.

166

# Writing a Personal Story

Now it is your turn to write a personal story about a dream of your own. *Sails in the Sky*, which begins on page 16 of this book, is written as if it was a personal story. Use these steps to help you write your personal story.

## Planning

Begin by studying the features of a **personal story**.

- A personal story tells a true or made-up story that happened to the writer.
- The writer uses the words I, me, or my.
- It shows the writer's feelings about the experience.

Use the chart you filled out to help you select a topic. Be sure your topic is small enough to write about in one paragraph.

## Composing

Now it is time to write your first draft.

- Brainstorm your ideas with a classmate.
- Begin your paragraph with a **topic sentence**. This tells the main idea of your paragraph.
- Add some details that help tell more about the main idea.
- Write your events in order.
- Include the characters, time, and place of the experience you are writing about.
- Tell how you felt about what happened.

**MAKING ALL THE CONNECTIONS**

## Proofreading Marks

∧ add

𝄐 take out

≡ capitalize

/ lower case

Lee decides this detail does not tell about the main idea.

These two sentences have the same naming part: *I*. Lee puts them together to make one long sentence.

# Revising

Now that you have written your first draft, your next step is to revise your writing. The following checklist will help you.

**Revising Checklist**
- ✔ Have I included all the features of a personal story?
- ✔ Does the story tell about the characters, time, and place of the experience?
- ✔ Can I combine two short sentences that have the same naming parts?

Lee has written a first draft of her personal story. She is going to revise it. Lee uses the Revising Checklist, and uses proofreading marks to show her corrections.

> I've always dreemed of being an artist, but my first art class was a nightmare. ~~It was the day of my first ballet class.~~ I got paint on my nose, and ~~I got~~ glue on my hands. the teacher said that I really got into my work. I felt so dumb.

# Proofreading

Now that you have revised your first draft, your next step is to revise punctuation and spelling. The following checklist will help you.

168

Lee looks at her personal story again. She checks errors in spelling, punctuation, and capitalization. Lee uses the Proofreading Checklist to help her.

> dreamed
>
> I've always ~~dreemed~~ of being an artist, but my first art class was a nightmare. It was the day of my first ~~ballet class~~. I got paint on my nose, and I ~~got~~ glue on my hands. the teacher said that I really got into my work. I felt so dumb.

Lee fixes a spelling mistake.

Lee puts a period at the end of a sentence.

Lee uses a capital letter at the beginning of a sentence.

Now it is your turn to revise. Ask a classmate to point out parts of your work that can be made better. Then use his or her ideas and the checklists to help you revise.

## Presenting

Make a neat final copy of your personal story. Use these ideas to share it with your class.

**Reading Aloud**   Read your personal story to the class. Read slowly so that everyone can hear.

**Making a Class Reader**   Put everyone's personal story together in a class scrapbook.

**169**

# PART THREE

# Mysteries

Something is there
    there on the stair
        coming down
            coming down
                stepping with care.
            Coming down
                coming down
                slinkety-sly.
Something is coming and wants to get by.

*Something Is There*
by Lilian Moore

---◆---

The world is full of mysteries. In these stories you'll
meet people who are looking for answers. You'll
also discover some answers for yourself. As you
read, think: What mysteries will you solve?

**171**

# Exploring Words About Mysteries

## Starting with What You Know

When you think of mysteries, what ideas come to mind? The words in the box below tell about mysteries. Use these words and words of you own to answer the questions after the box.

| | | |
|---|---|---|
| riddle | scary | discover |
| puzzling | explore | detective story |
| interesting | puzzle | search |

Some people might say that mysteries are scary. How would you describe a mystery? A mystery might be a kind of puzzle. What other kind of mystery could there be? Some people explore to solve a mystery. What else might people do to solve a mystery?

## Building a Word Map

The word map shows how some of the words in the box above go together. Think about words you can add to the map. Use words from the box and other words of your own.

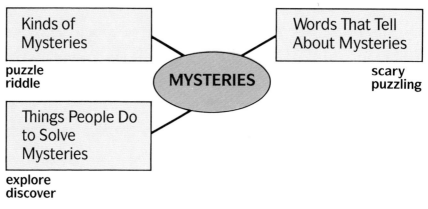

Kinds of Mysteries
puzzle
riddle

Words That Tell About Mysteries
scary
puzzling

MYSTERIES

Things People Do to Solve Mysteries
explore
discover

## Finishing a Story

Look at the story below. The story tells about a mystery at school. Some words are missing. Think of the words you would use to finish the story. Use the words from the box and word map in this lesson for ideas. Complete the story.

There was a big _____ at school today. It was Cathy. She would not laugh or smile or talk. It was a _____ mystery. Her friends wanted to _____ what was wrong. They asked Cathy, But she would not _____.

Tommy had a good idea. He told Cathy a joke. Cathy laughed. Tommy solved the _____. Cathy had braces on her teeth.

Now Cathy is happy again. She laughs, _____, and _____ just like before.

Share your story with your class. How were the stories different? What words did your classmates use?

## As You Read

In this part of the book, you will read about mysteries and the people who solve them. Keeping a Reader's Log will help you remember important thoughts, ideas, and words. As you read, make notes in your log. You could begin your Reader's Log with the word map. Add new words to the map as you find them.

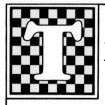

# THEME SETTER

Sam often hears harmonica music playing in his apartment building. Where could the music be coming from? Sam and his brother decide to find out.

by Ezra Jack Keats

The rain fell steadily. It beat against the windows, softening the sounds of the city. As Sam gazed out, he heard someone in the building playing a harmonica. It filled him with sad and lonely feelings—like the rain outside. He had heard that music before. Each time it was different. "Who's that playing?" Sam wondered.

Sam went into the hall and listened. No music. His little brother Ben tagged along.

They walked down to the floor below. A dog was barking—real mean—in Apt. 9. Next door a mother sang softly to her crying baby. At Apt. 7, not a sound.

Down another flight. The hall light was broken. At Apt. 6, there was a ball game on TV. It sounded like a million people were in there cheering.

**174**

Apt. 5—loud, juicy snoring. Ben bumped into an old, worn-out mattress. "That snorer sure's enjoying his new one," Sam said. Apt. 4—more yelling.

Finally, the ground floor. Apt. 3 was quiet. Just a container of milk outside the door. They stopped in front of Apt. 2—Betsy's door. Sam thought. "Maybe she'll come out and I'll say hello to her." He decided to hang around. "Let's rest a little," he said. They sat on the steps.

But no Betsy. And no music. "C'mon, let's go home," said Ben.

As they turned to go upstairs, Sam noticed that the container of milk was gone!

He went over to take a good look. The door was open a little. He peeked in.

**175**

"WELL?" A sharp voice startled Sam.

Sam could make out a figure at a table. It was the blind man's apartment! "Come on in, you two! What's the matter—scared?"

Sam shut the door and sat down.

"I know about you boys. You live upstairs," said the man. "I know something else about you, Sam."

"What?" whispered Sam.

"You like the little girl across the hall. The way you slow down when you pass her door. The real nice way you say 'Hi, Betsy' and she says 'Hi Sam.'" Ben giggled.

Sam jumped up. He yelled. "I know about you too. You sit around here, finding out other people's secrets!"

The man's face took on a faraway look. "I know plenty, young fellow. I know when it rains, when it snows, what people are cooking, and what they think they are fighting about. Secrets? You want to hear some secrets? Listen."

He stood up suddenly, raised his harmonica to his mouth, and began to play. He played purples and grays and rain and smoke and the sounds of night. Sam sat quietly and listened. He felt that all the sights and sounds and colors from outside had come into the room and were floating around. He floated with them. Ben's eyes were closed, and he was smiling.

After a while, Sam turned to the man and said, "Would you like to take a walk with us tomorrow?" The music became so soft and quiet they could barely hear it.

Then the room filled with wild happy music. It bounced from wall to wall. Sam and Ben looked at each other. They couldn't wait for tomorrow.

## Thinking About the Theme

**1.** Do you think Sam was more excited by solving the mystery of where the music came from or by making a new friend?

**2.** Do you think that there are some mysteries that might be better left unsolved?

# Understanding Fact and Opinion

## Starting with What You Know

THAT ONE HAS A NICE CABINET.

THAT'S A GOOD PRICE!

I LIKE THE BIG SCREEN.

IT'S COOL!

SALE

THIS MODEL HAS A 21-INCH SCREEN. THE CABINET IS 29 INCHES WIDE AND 25 INCHES DEEP.

Do you think the family will buy the TV? Why?

## Thinking About Fact and Opinion

A **fact** is something that can be checked or shown to be true. An **opinion** is what a person thinks about something. It can't be shown to be true or false. In the picture, who is giving facts? Who is giving opinions?

In articles, you may see words such as *nice*, *wonderful*, *big*, and *better*. These words tell you someone is giving an opinion. Read the paragraph at the top of the next page. Which sentences give facts? Which give opinions?

Department stores are nice places to go shopping for a television set. These stores have many different kinds of TV sets, and they have sales clerks to help you. Big TVs are really the best kind, but some small TVs are good, too. Department stores sell more color TV sets than black and white sets.

You probably said that the first and third sentences give opinions. The others state facts.

## Practice

Read the paragraph. Tell which sentences give facts and which give opinions.

Thomas Edison was an American inventor. He was born in Ohio and lived from 1847 to 1931. In those days, Ohio was a wonderful state in which to live. Edison invented the electric light bulb and the phonograph. The phonograph was his best invention because it plays music.

## As You Read

Ask yourself these questions:
- Which details can be checked or shown to be true?
- Which words show that the writer is giving an opinion?

Use what you know about fact and opinion as you read the two selections that follow. Use the side notes to help you.

**You probably use electricity every day, but do you really understand how it works? In this article you can explore the mystery of electricity for yourself.**

# ELECTRICITY:
# What Makes It Work?

## by Anne Cappy

Flip a switch and a light goes on. It's simple, right? Wrong! Every time you flip a light switch, you make billions of little electrons go to work for you. Uncountable hours of work have gone into providing you with the electricity you need to turn that light on. Without electricity you wouldn't have telephones, TV, video games, and many other things you use every day.

This is a fact. It can be checked.

### What Is Electricity?
Have you ever gotten a shock when you touched a doorknob, or seen sparks fly when you brushed your hair? That's electricity.

What you already know helps you understand electricity.

**180**

Electricity is a type of energy that gives things the power to work. This energy comes from electrons. Scientists have learned how to use electrons to produce electricity.

## How Does It Work?

It takes billions of electrons to make electricity operate. Electrons move through an electric wire in much the same way water moves through a garden hose. Turning the knob pushes the water through the hose. Pushing electrons makes electricity move through the wire.

This point explains how electricity works.

The machine that pushes the billions of electrons through the wire is called a generator. The wire from the generator goes to your home and into a center that controls the flow of electricity. The center is either a fuse box or a circuit breaker.

The fuse box controls how much electricity you use. If you try to use too much, you will "blow a fuse," and the electricity from that fuse will be cut off. A circuit breaker controls electricity in a different way. It does not let you use too much. It cuts off the flow before there's an overload. If you did not have a fuse box or circuit breaker, your electric wires could overheat and start a fire!

From the fuse box or circuit breaker, the wires go inside your walls to light switches and sockets. Turning on the light switch lets the electricity flow to the light, and the light goes on. When you put a plug into a socket, electricity comes to the socket. But it doesn't flow into the lamp until the switch is turned on.

### How Can We Use It?

These are facts about sound.

Besides turning on lights, we can use electricity to carry sound. Sound is made by a type of vibration called a sound wave. The electricity in a telephone picks up the sound waves from the speaker on one end and carries them to the receiver on the other end. The electricity moves so fast that you can hardly notice the time it takes to travel from one place to another.

When you turn on your TV, you get something very nice. You get both light and sound. Again, it is electricity that makes this possible, allowing you to see and hear your favorite shows!

Here the writer gives an opinion. "Nice" can't be checked or shown to be a fact.

## What Does It Do?

There are two opinions in this part. Think about why they can't be checked or shown to be true or false.

Electricity is wonderful. It makes so many things possible. Most of our food comes from farms that use machines that run on electricity. Most of our clothes are made in factories that need electricity to operate.

Life would be pretty boring without electricity. We have gotten used to all the things it can do. Scientists have worked for hundreds of years to bring electricity to us, and are still working to find new and better ways to produce the electricity that makes so many things happen.

## A Reader Says

*I bet someday electricity will be so important that everyone will drive electric cars.*

How did you feel about the article?

# After You Read

## Thinking About What You Read

**1.** Why do you think overloading a wire with electricity would start a fire?

**2.** Why do you think electricity doesn't flow into a lamp until the switch is turned on?

**3.** How do you know that life would be difficult without electricity?

**4.** Do you think scientists know everything there is to know about electricity? Why or why not?

## Thinking About How You Read

How did knowing the difference between fact and opinion help you to find important facts about electricity in this article?

## Sharing and Listening

Suppose you could use electricity for only one item in your home. Which item would you choose? Share your ideas of what life would be like without electricity. Listen as your classmates share their ideas.

## Writing

Suppose there were an electrical power failure and no electrical things worked for one whole day. Write a paragraph telling about that day and the things you could not do or had to do in a different way because there was no electricity.

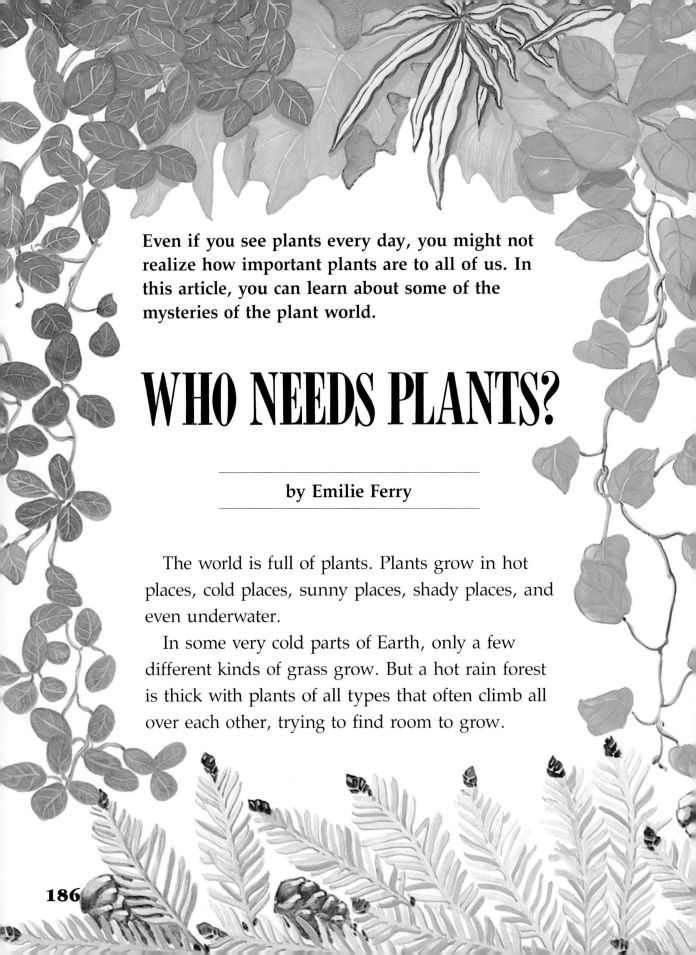

Even if you see plants every day, you might not realize how important plants are to all of us. In this article, you can learn about some of the mysteries of the plant world.

# WHO NEEDS PLANTS?

**by Emilie Ferry**

The world is full of plants. Plants grow in hot places, cold places, sunny places, shady places, and even underwater.

In some very cold parts of Earth, only a few different kinds of grass grow. But a hot rain forest is thick with plants of all types that often climb all over each other, trying to find room to grow.

One kind of plant that grows underwater is so very tiny that two hundred of them in a row would only be one inch long. Other plants, like redwood trees, grow to be as tall as three hundred and fifty feet. Redwood trees are the tallest trees in the world.

Some plants live a long time. Some redwood trees are over one thousand years old, but they aren't as old as one kind of pine tree. The oldest of these pine trees is about five thousand years old. Other plants, however, live a very short time. There are some very small plants that live for less than an hour.

With so many plants in the world, most of us see them very often, and we don't always realize how important they are. We couldn't live without plants.

Plants provide food for people and animals, and if all plants disappeared from Earth, we would run out of food very soon.

We eat all parts of plants. We eat the roots of carrots and the stems of celery. We eat the leaves of many plants. When we eat green onions, we're eating a part of the leaves. Some vegetables we eat are flowers, such as the cauliflower.

When we think of eating fruit, we may think of apples, bananas, peaches, and melons. But the part of any plant that holds the seed is a fruit. When we eat bread or any food made with flour, we're eating the fruit of different kinds of grass, such as wheat or oats. Even corn is the fruit of a very large kind of grass.

Chickens, cows, and other animals eat food from plants, then the animals, in turn, provide us with food such as milk, eggs, and meat.

Plants provide many other things that we use, such as wax, cotton for clothes, and natural oil for soap. We use things made with wood from trees all the time. Many homes and other buildings are made with wood and some people even wear wooden shoes. Trees also provide paper for books and film for taking pictures.

Plants help us in other ways. They keep soil from washing or blowing away, and they keep the air fresh for us to breathe.

People get pleasure from plants. Everyone enjoys the shade of trees on a hot day. People who work with plants in a garden get pleasure from seeing natural things grow. And the natural beauty of plants gives us all a lot of pleasure, too.

Plants are wonderful things. We couldn't get along without them.

## A Reader Says

*I never knew that wheat and oats are really fruits just like apples and bananas. I would like to learn more about the different parts of plants.*

How did you feel about the article?

# After You Read

## Thinking About What You Read

1. Why do you think some trees can live to be 5,000 years old?
2. Why do you think some plants grow underwater?
3. Why do you think some plants grow 350 feet high and others can hardly be seen because they are so tiny?
4. How do you know plants are important to life on Earth?

## Thinking About How You Read

How did knowing the difference between fact and opinion help you understand the author's opinions about plants?

## Sharing and Listening

What would life be like without trees or plants anywhere? Share your thoughts and feelings about this with your classmates. Listen as your classmates share their ideas.

## Writing

Choose one plant. Write a list telling all the benefits we receive from that plant.

# GROW
## YOUR OWN PLANT

You have just read an article about plants. Maybe now you would like to grow a plant of your own. It's easy to do. Just remember to take good care of your plant so that it will grow.

In order to grow your own plant, you will need a cutting from a plant, a paper cup, soil, and water. Follow these directions and you will soon have a beautiful, healthy plant.

**1.** First ask your parent or a friend if you can have a cutting from one of their plants. A cutting is a twig or leaf that has been cut from a growing plant. Taking a cutting will not hurt a plant. It will continue to grow.

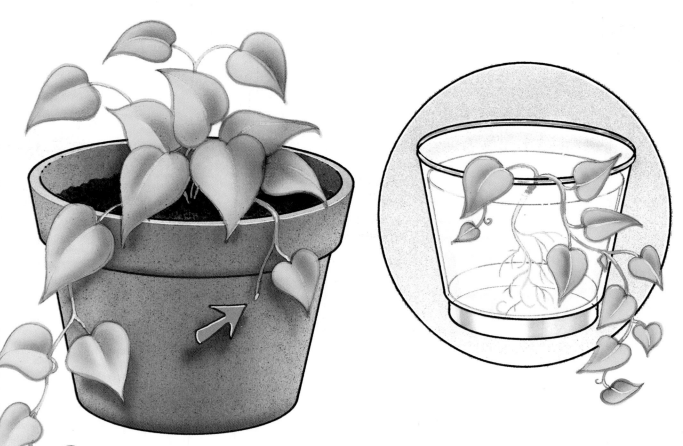

**2.** To take a cutting, break off a twig with at least one leaf. You might want to look at the stem of the plant. The stem grows up from the bottom of the plant and supports it. If the stem has small bumps, break off a twig that is growing from under one of the bumps.

**3.** Now fill the paper cup with water, and place the twig in it. Make sure the leaves are not underwater. Leave the cup in a place where it will get light, and add water when needed.

**4.** In a few days, the twig will have grown roots. Roots hold the plant in place under the ground. They take in water and minerals from the soil. This food helps the plant grow.

**193**

**5.** Once the twig has several roots, take it out of the water and wash the cup.

**6.** Now make two small holes in the bottom of the cup so water can drain out.

**7.** Next, fill the cup about half full with soil, and put in the twig. Stick the roots into the soil.

**8.** Water the plant just a little, and add more dirt until you almost fill the cup.

**9.** Add more water until the soil is damp, and smooth it out with your fingers.

**10.** Finally, place a small plate under the cup, and put your plant near a window. Be sure to water it whenever the soil gets dry. Now you are ready to watch your young plant grow.

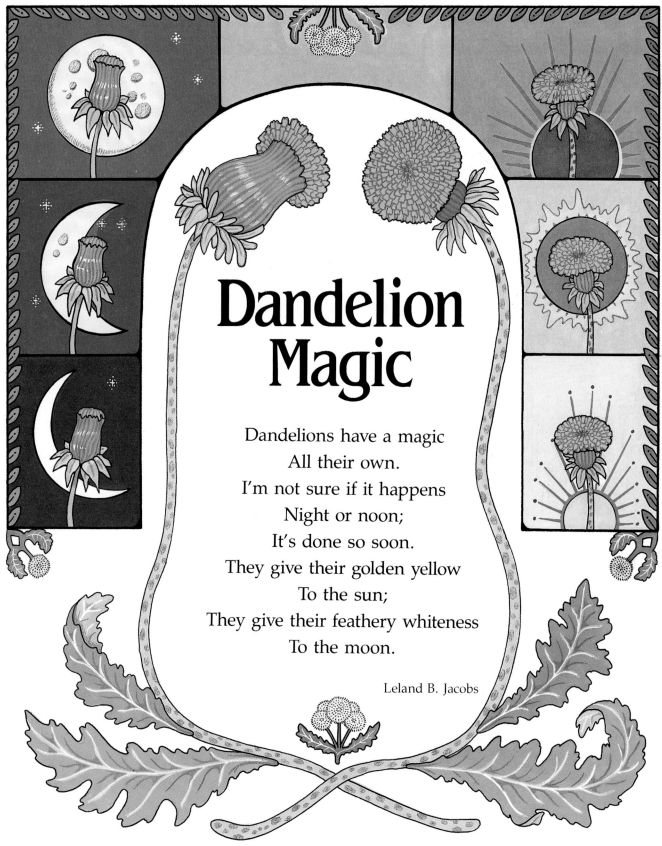

# Dandelion Magic

Dandelions have a magic
All their own.
I'm not sure if it happens
Night or noon;
It's done so soon.
They give their golden yellow
To the sun;
They give their feathery whiteness
To the moon.

Leland B. Jacobs

195

# Understanding Fantasy

### Starting with What You Know

What story do you know about an animal who talks? What story do you know about a person who can do something like fly like a bird?

### Thinking About Fantasy

The kind of story you just thought about could never really happen. It is a kind of make-believe story called **fantasy**. A fantasy has four parts, like other fiction stories.

Characters: These are the people or animals in the story.

Setting: This is the place and time when the story happens.

Plot: These are the important events in the story. In some stories, two or three events make up the plot.

Outcome: This is the way the story ends. In many stories, the main characters solve a problem.

In a fantasy, the characters are not like real people or animals. The setting of the story might be a strange place. Many of the actions that make up the plot are make-believe. In the outcome, a character might solve a problem, but the solution might be something that could not happen in real life.

## Before You Read

Look at the name of the story, and look at the pictures. Try to guess what will happen in the story.

## As You Read

Stop after every page. Think about what you have read so far. Try to guess what will happen next. Ask yourself these questions as you read. The questions with the blue diamonds are for any kind of fiction. The questions with red diamonds are for fantasy.

Characters: ◆ Who are the characters?

◆ How are the characters unusual?

Setting: ◆ Where and when does the story happen?

Plot: ◆ What are the important events?

◆ What make-believe events happen?

Outcome: ◆ What problem does it solve at the end?

Apply what you know about reading fantasy stories as you read the two fantasy selections that follow. Use the side notes to help you.

Carruthers is usually a cheerful bear. Why he's been acting grumpy lately is a mystery to Eugene and Emily.

# What's the Matter with Carruthers?

## by James Marshall

One fall morning Emily Pig and her friend Eugene were enjoying a stroll in the park.

"What beautiful weather," said Emily. "I'm sure we are going to meet some of our friends here today."

"That would be very nice," said Eugene.

Sure enough, they came upon their old friend Carruthers sitting alone on a wooden bench, busy staring at the falling leaves.

Emily, Eugene, and Carruthers are the main characters.

The animals talk to each other like people. This makes the story a fantasy.

"Good morning, Carruthers," they both called out in their most cheerful voices.

"Good morning," said Carruthers. But his voice was far from cheerful. It was the kind of "good morning" that really means, "Go away, I want to be left alone."

Carruthers has a problem.

"I'm worried about Carruthers," Emily whispered to Eugene. "He hasn't been himself lately. He's so grumpy and unpleasant."

"It's not like Carruthers to be unpleasant," Eugene whispered back. "He always has a kind word for everyone."

Leaving Carruthers to sit alone on his bench and stare at the falling leaves, Emily and Eugene went on with their stroll through the park.

"There must be something that we can do to cheer him up," said Emily. "If Carruthers keeps acting this way, he won't have any friends left."

"That's very true," said Eugene, "because no one likes a grouch."

So the two friends plopped down on a bench and thought long and hard.

"Well," Eugene said, "whenever I'm feeling grumpy, I listen to beautiful music."

"That gives me an idea," exclaimed Emily. "Come with me."

The two friends hurried home. In a few minutes, they were both back in the park. Emily had her tuba, and Eugene had his drum.

The setting is a park.

They found Carruthers still sitting in the same place. Ever so quietly, they tiptoed up behind him.

Emily played the tuba softly at first and then loudly, while Eugene tapped on his drum.

Carruthers put his paws to his ears and growled, "That is the worst noise I've ever heard in my life!"

Then he got up and walked away.

**200**

Emily and Eugene looked at each other. "Maybe we should have practiced more," said Eugene.

Emily sat down. "Just because we couldn't make Carruthers feel better with our music, we cannot give up. We must think of another way."

"Yes," agreed Eugene, "we must not give up."

So once again, they both thought long and hard.

"I know," said Emily, "let's ask him to have lunch with us."

"Of course! What a great idea," said Eugene. "Let's go to your house right away and send him an invitation."

Carruthers was an even bigger grouch when he came home and found the invitation to lunch. He did not feel like visiting—but what bear can stay away from food? So of course he went.

At Emily's house, Carruthers plopped down in the very best chair and watched as Eugene helped Emily serve lunch.

Now the setting changes to Emily's house. You know a real pig could not have a house like this.

**201**

"It's another beautiful day, isn't it?" said Emily, trying to start a friendly talk.

"Not really," said Carruthers.

"You must enjoy taking a stroll in the park," said Eugene.

"No, not really," said Carruthers.

"My, how lovely your fur looks today, Carruthers," said Emily.

"I've never cared for it," said Carruthers.

Emily and Eugene didn't know what else to say, since Carruthers was acting so unpleasant.

When Carruthers finished eating, he said, "Thank you for serving lunch, but I must leave now. I need to get some fresh air."

"Then why don't we all go for a drive?" said Eugene.

"What a good idea!" exclaimed Emily. "I'm sure a ride out in the country will make Carruthers feel great."

And before Carruthers could say anything at all, he found himself sitting in the back seat of Emily's car.

Very soon the three friends were sailing through the open countryside.

"There's nothing like a drive in the country on a sunny day to cheer a person up," called out Eugene.

"The countryside gives me hay fever," was all Carruthers would say.

Emily and Eugene are trying to help Carruthers. Think about why he is being so grouchy.

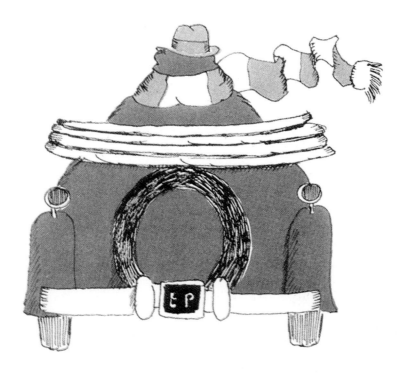

After a little while, Carruthers said, "I think it's time to go home. I'm not having a good time riding through the countryside."

Emily and Eugene were both upset. "I was hopeful that this drive would cheer him up," said Emily, "but Carruthers isn't one little bit better."

"I know," said Eugene. "I don't think there's anything else we can do but take him home."

Imagine what Emily and Eugene might try next.

On the way home no one spoke.

When they pulled up in front of Carruthers's house, Emily had an idea. "Carruthers," she said, "look at all those leaves in your front yard. I think we should help you rake them."

This was an idea that Carruthers did not like at all. It was not his idea of fun to rake leaves, but he went to find three rakes and a big basket.

"I don't see why we should help Carruthers rake his leaves," said Eugene.

"Sometimes keeping very busy is a good way to forget about feeling grumpy," Emily said.

When Carruthers came back, they went to work and kept very busy. Emily and Carruthers would rake leaves into the basket, and Eugene would put them into a pile. Soon the pile was very high.

"If we hurry," said Emily, "we will be finished in time for dinner."

But Carruthers was beginning to slow down.

He started to yawn. A small yawn at first, which he covered with his paw. Then a much bigger yawn. And then—a great big bear yawn.

Think about what time of year it is. You may already know something about bears that helps you solve Carruthers's problem.

All of a sudden, Carruthers plopped headfirst into the huge pile of leaves.

"Oh my!" cried Eugene. "What in the world has happened?"

The two friends quickly cleared away the pile of leaves and uncovered Carruthers.

"He's asleep!" they both exclaimed.

"So that is why Carruthers has been such a terrible grouch lately," said Emily. "Why didn't we think of this before? He forgot that it was time for his long winter's sleep."

Now Emily and Eugene know what was wrong.

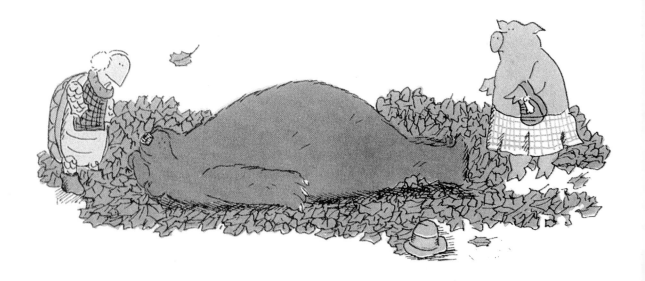

"Of course. Now I understand," said Eugene. "Carruthers is usually tucked away in bed many days ago. No wonder he has been so impossible to be around."

"There is no use waking him now," said Emily. "He'll be asleep for the rest of the winter, so it's up to us to get him into bed."

"That will be the hardest job yet," said Eugene.

After a lot of huffing and puffing, they lifted the sleeping Carruthers, who was just beginning to snore, into a small wagon and pulled it into the house.

When they got to Carruthers's bedroom, they huffed and puffed and ever so slowly put him under the snug winter covers. Emily pulled his nightcap down around his ears. Eugene set the alarm clock for spring and pulled down the shades.

They are able to help Carruthers after all. Ask yourself if this could really happen.

"Good night, Carruthers," whispered Emily, and she gave him a kiss on the cheek. "Sleep tight, and we'll see you in the spring when you will be your old sweet self again."

## A Reader Says

*I think Emily and Eugene should have left Carruthers alone. They meant well, but maybe he would have gone to sleep sooner if they weren't there.*

How did you feel about the story?

# After You Read

## Thinking About What You Read

**1.** Why do you think Carruthers was in such a bad mood?

**2.** Why do you think Carruthers found tuba and drum music unpleasant?

**3.** How do you know that Emily and Eugene care about Carruthers?

**4.** Do you think Emily and Eugene had a good time with Carruthers? Why or why not?

## Thinking About How You Read

How did understanding about fantasy help you to see the funny things that happened in this story?

## Sharing and Listening

Suppose you had a friend who started acting grumpy. Would you try to figure out what was wrong? How would you solve the mystery? Think about what you would do. Share your ideas with your classmates. Listen as your classmates share their ideas.

## Writing

Your friend is in a bad mood. You decide to write a funny story or song to cheer your friend up. Write a funny story or song. Share your story or song with your classmates. If you wish, draw a picture to help cheer up your friend, too.

**Kenneth the rooster is Cunningham's best friend.
What would Cunningham ever do without him?**

# Cunningham's Rooster

### by Barbara Brenner

There was once a cat named Cunningham who wrote music. He made up songs for singing and songs for dancing and melodies just for listening.

First he would hear a song in his head, and then he would play it on the piano. Later he would write down the notes in his big black notebook, so he wouldn't forget how the songs went.

They were wonderful songs, too. The only
trouble was, nobody heard them, because
Cunningham lived all alone except for his goldfish,
and everyone knows that a goldfish has no ear for
music.

It was beginning to get Cunningham down. He
wished he could find a friend who really enjoyed
music.

"What good is a song if there's nobody around
to hear it?" he asked himself.

One evening as he sat playing the piano and
wishing that a goldfish *did* have an ear for music,
there was a pecking sound at the patio door. He
looked up to see who it was and saw that it was a
rooster.

"My name is Kenneth," the rooster said, as he
opened the patio door with his beak. "I was
walking by, and I stopped to tell you that I really
like that song you're playing. It's so mellow."

Cunningham couldn't have been more pleased.
"There's more where that came from," he said.
"Why don't you step inside?"

Kenneth did step inside, and Cunningham
played for him every song he had ever written—
songs for singing and songs for dancing and
melodies that were just for listening. When the
music was over, Kenneth flapped his wings and
clucked with pleasure. Cunningham knew then that
he and the rooster were going to be good friends.

"Stay with me," he said to Kenneth, "and you
can hear my new melodies and give me Inspiration."

"What's Inspiration?" Kenneth wanted to know.

"It's the feeling I get that makes me hear songs
in my head," Cunningham explained.

"Well," said Kenneth, "I'll sure try to give you
some Inspiration, but what will you give me?"

"A roost of your own and all the brown rice you can eat," said Cunningham.

"Agreed," said Kenneth quickly. "It will be a pleasure to stay with you!" He picked out a roost in Cunningham's bookcase and went to sleep, happy that he wasn't going to live in a barnyard anymore.

Having someone to listen to his music changed everything for Cunningham. Now every day found him happy and hard at work, making up songs and then writing them down in his big notebook.

As for Kenneth, every day found him sitting under the piano, listening with pleasure to Cunningham's songs, or pecking and scratching around outside in the dirt, talking in riddles to the bugs before he ate them.

"Do bugs look like notes of music, or do notes of music look like bugs?" Kenneth loved to ask.

One day Cunningham was watching Kenneth pecking and scratching in the dirt. Suddenly he shouted, "I have an Inspiration! I will make up some music about Kenneth. It will have three parts to it and I will call it 'The Rooster Rhapsody'!"

He sat right down at the piano and began writing. The first part was all about Kenneth. It was about how Kenneth looked, the things Kenneth did, and what Kenneth was like. There were light sounds in it—like the way Kenneth clucked when he whispered to bugs and the cheerful little dance that Kenneth did when he was scratching in the dirt. It was a wonderful song, as light as feathers and as happy as the crow of a rooster in the morning.

When Kenneth heard the beginning of the rhapsody, he loved it.

"It's me all over!" he said.

Cunningham was pleased, too, because he knew it was by far the best music he had ever written. He decided to take it to the city and show it to an Important Music Person.

Before he left, Cunningham filled Kenneth's dish with brown rice and had a quiet little talk with him.

"Kenneth," he said, "I understand there's a hungry opossum who lives back in the woods. She has many teeth and would like nothing better than to eat a fat rooster. So promise me that you won't go out this evening after dark."

"Okay, I promise," said Kenneth.

All went well during the day, but as evening fell, fireflies began coming close to the patio door, and they winked at Kenneth from outside. The moon rose and made the trees look like shadows and the shadows look like trees.

The fireflies winked at Kenneth again and again, until he began feeling restless. He longed to talk in riddles to the fireflies and he wanted to visit his old barnyard friends.

At last Kenneth said, "This is the kind of night when a rooster could forget a promise."

He opened the patio door with his beak and took a step out into the dark night. Then he took another step and another.

He clucked softly to the fireflies, "Do bugs look
like notes of music, or do notes of music look
like . . .?"

But before Kenneth had even gotten through
the beginning of his riddle, the hungry opossum
crept quietly out of the shadows, and suddenly . . .
pounce!

When Cunningham came home he was filled
with happiness because the Important Music Person
had liked his work and had said that it wouldn't be
at all surprising if "The Rooster Rhapsody" made
Cunningham famous. Cunningham couldn't wait
to tell Kenneth.

But Kenneth couldn't be found.

Cunningham went to the kitchen and saw that
the dish of brown rice was there, but Kenneth
wasn't. He wasn't in the bookcase or under the
piano or in any other favorite place.

Finally Cunningham took a flashlight and went out into the backyard. Cunningham could see by the light of the flashlight the tracks of an opossum and four golden feathers from a rooster's tail. It didn't take long for Cunningham to guess what had happened.

It was a sad cat who walked back into the house that night. He put the flashlight away and sat down at the piano. He thought of all the good times that were over and all the sad years ahead.

Slowly Cunningham began to make up a new part to his rhapsody. Some of it sounded as restless as a spring night, some of it sounded like the pounce of an animal, and some of it was slow and low and full of the sadness of a lost friend.

"This is the second part of my 'Rooster Rhapsody,'" said Cunningham with tears in his eyes.

"I guess it is the last song I will ever write, because my Inspiration is gone. What am I without my Inspiration?" he asked himself. "What's a cat without his work?"

Cunningham closed the piano and put away the big black notebook and the felt marker. Then he lay down on his bed and pulled the quilt over his head.

Those were terrible days, full of sadness. The milk went bad on the back porch, dust stood on the piano, and the goldfish bowl began to get dirty.

Then one morning there was a pecking at the patio door.

"Come in," whispered Cunningham, without even opening his eyes.

A moment later he heard a scratching sound, and the next thing he knew someone was pulling the quilt away from his head.

Cunningham opened his eyes, and there was Kenneth!

"Dear friend," cried Cunningham, "is it really you?"

"No one else," clucked Kenneth.

"I thought you were gone forever," said Cunningham. "I saw opossum tracks and rooster's feathers—"

"No, no, old friend," said Kenneth. "Remember—an opossum can pounce, but a rooster can roost! That's what I did—went up a tree and lost nothing but a few tail feathers."

"But why didn't you come back before now?" asked Cunningham.

"I guess I should have," Kenneth said, "but it was such a lovely spring night, and I wanted to visit some old friends in the barnyard."

Cunningham didn't have the heart to be angry with Kenneth. Also, at that moment, a new song came into his head. He blew the dust off the piano and began to play, while Kenneth cleaned the goldfish bowl.

What a wonderful song Cunningham wrote! A joyful song, full of mellow notes that were as golden as Kenneth's tail feathers. It was a lovely song about a friend who had come back and the happiness that had come with him. It was a song from the heart, a joyful song for everyone who ever had a friend and for everyone who ever loved music.

Now the three parts of "The Rooster Rhapsody" were finished. After Cunningham wrote down the last notes, he played the whole thing through. . . .

The first part was joyful and as light as feathers, the second part was slow and low and filled with sadness, and the last part was lovely and mellow and golden.

Each song alone was fine, but all together they made the most beautiful music ever.

All the animals came out of the woods to hear "The Rooster Rhapsody." Soon the whole backyard was filled with animals, and every animal who heard the music went away filled with happiness.

As for Kenneth, he was so happy that he threw back his head and began to crow. Cunningham wrote down the sound of Kenneth's crowing, and it became the last notes of "The Rooster Rhapsody."

The rhapsody *did* make Cunningham famous. It made Kenneth famous, also, because every time "The Rooster Rhapsody" was played, someone would ask who had been the Inspiration for such wonderful music. Then someone else would always remember and tell the story of Cunningham's rooster.

## A Reader Says

◆━━━━━━━━━━━━━━━━━━━━━━━━━━━━━━━━━━◆

*It turned out to be a good thing that Kenneth disappeared, because it inspired Cunningham to write the rest of the Rhapsody and make it beautiful.*

How did you feel about the story?

◆━━━━━━━━━━━━━━━━━━━━━━━━━━━━━━━━━━◆

# After You Read

## Thinking About What You Read

**1.** Why do you think Cunningham needed a friend to enjoy his music?

**2.** How do you know Cunningham was fond of Kenneth?

**3.** Do you think it was smart of Kenneth to go outside after Cunningham had warned him about the opposum? Why or why not?

**4.** Why do you think Kenneth took a long time returning to Cunningham's house?

## Thinking About How You Read

How did understanding about fantasy help you guess the kinds of things that animals like Cunningham and Kenneth would do in this story?

## Sharing and Listening

In the story you just read, Kenneth, the rooster, disappears. Why do you think Cunningham did not search for him? If you were Cunningham, how would you solve the mystery of Kenneth's disappearance? Share your ideas with your classmates. Listen as your classmates share their ideas.

## Writing

Kenneth loved to tell silly riddles to insects, bugs, and fireflies. Make believe you are Kenneth. Write a silly poem or riddle to an insect, bug, or firefly.

**George W. Allen knows a lot about his hero, George Washington. But what our first President ate for breakfast is a mystery even George might not be able to solve.**

# George Washington's Breakfast

◆

## by Jean Fritz

George W. Allen was proud of two things. His name and his birthday.

George was named for George Washington. And he had the same birthday. February 22.

It made him feel almost related, he said.

It made him want to know everything there was to know about George Washington.

Already he knew quite a lot. He knew that Washington was a general and lived in Virginia and was six feet tall and married to Martha and was the first President of the United States.

He also knew that Washington rode two horses in the war, Blueskin and Nelson, but Nelson was his favorite because he was so steady in gunfire.

Then one day at breakfast George Allen thought of something he didn't know. George's mother and father had gone to work, and his grandmother was frying eggs at the kitchen stove.

"Grandma," George said, "what did George Washington eat for breakfast?"

"Search me," his grandmother said. "That was before my time." She put a plate of fried eggs in front of George.

"Well," he said, "if I find out, will you do one thing for me?"

"What's that?"

"Will you cook me George Washington's breakfast?"

George's grandmother looked at the clock on the kitchen wall. "George," she said, "you'll be late for school."

"But will you?" George insisted. "Will you cook me George Washington's breakfast?"

"I'll cook anything," she said, "as long as you hurry."

After school that day George Allen went to the library. Miss Willing, the librarian, smiled when she saw him come in the door. "I wonder what that Allen boy wants to know now," she thought.

George walked up to the desk. "Miss Willing," he said, "do you know what George Washington ate for breakfast?"

Miss Willing could hardly remember what *she'd* had for breakfast that morning, but like George, she liked to find out answers.

Together George and Miss Willing went to the encyclopedia and looked under *W*. "Washington, George." The encyclopedia said Washington was born in 1732, married in 1759, elected President in 1789, and died in 1799. It told all about the years when he took trips and fought battles and did other important things. But it didn't say what he did every day. It didn't mention his breakfasts.

Miss Willing took George to the card catalogue, where information about every book in the whole library was written down on a separate card, with a number or letter that told where you could find the book. George liked opening the little drawers of the catalogue and finding the right drawer and flipping through the cards until he found what he wanted. There were seven books about George Washington. Most of them were in the section of the library marked *B* for Biography.

George picked out four books to take home, and Miss Willing promised that she would look at the rest.

That night after supper George gave his father a book to read, and he gave his mother a book to read.

George kept the other two books for himself. All evening George and his mother and father read.

George was very excited when he found out that Washington liked to count things. George liked to count things too. George had counted how many steps there were between his house and the school. And there was Washington back in the 1700's counting steps too! It made George feel more related than ever.

But there wasn't a word about Washington's breakfasts, and the way George figured it, Washington must have eaten breakfast more than 24,000 times.

Then all at once Mrs. Allen looked up. "Listen to this," she said. "This book says that in Washington's time breakfast in Virginia usually consisted of cold turkey, cold meat, fried hominy, toast, cider, ham, bread and butter, tea, coffee and chocolate."

George Allen felt his mouth beginning to water. He grinned and looked at his grandmother.

"Humph!" his grandmother scoffed. "Notice the book said what was *usual* in Virginia. Everyone knows George Washington was an unusual man. No telling what he ate."

A little later Mr. Allen looked up from his book. "Guess what?" he said. "It says here that people in Washington's day didn't eat a real breakfast. Instead they had lunch at ten o'clock in the morning."

George Allen's grandmother grinned and looked at George.

"Doesn't mean a thing," George said. "That book's talking about Washington's day. Not about George Washington."

The day the Allens finished reading their four books was a Saturday, a nice, sunny spring Saturday. George went back to the library. Miss Willing suggested that they find out what some of George Washington's friends had to say.

First they read from the diary of John Adams, the second President of the United States. John Adams wrote that George Washington ruined his teeth when he was a boy by cracking walnuts in his mouth.

Thomas Jefferson, the third President of the United States, wrote that Washington was the best horseman of his age.

General Lafayette, who helped Washington fight the Revolutionary War, wrote that George Washington wore a size 13 shoe and had the biggest hands he'd ever seen.

No one mentioned if George Washington ever ate or not.

Day after day George and his mother and father and Miss Willing read. Then one day Miss Willing said the reading was over. There were no more books in the library about George Washington. Of course there were bigger libraries, she pointed out. George could go to one of them.

But George had a different idea. "We'll go to Washington's home in Mount Vernon, Virginia," he said, "where George Washington's breakfasts were actually cooked."

The next weekend George and Mr. and Mrs. Allen got in the car. They asked George's grandmother to come, but she said, no, she'd cook, but she wouldn't look. Besides, she was glad to get rid of them, she said. She could clean the attic without anyone poking around trying to rescue things that should be thrown out.

At Mount Vernon George and his mother and father went right to the kitchen. They walked on the same path that Washington had walked on, and every time George put his feet down, he thought of Washington's size 13's in the same spot.

The kitchen was in a separate building at the side of the house. It was a large room with a big brick fireplace at one end and brass pots and iron pots and griddles and pans and ladles hanging on the walls. George held his breath. It was at that very fireplace, he told himself, that Washington's breakfasts had been cooked. The food may actually have been in some of those very pots and pans. Suddenly George felt so related to Washington that goose pimples broke out on his arm.

He turned to a guard in uniform standing at the
door. "Can you tell me," George said, "what
George Washington ate for breakfast?"

The guard spoke as if he were reciting a lesson.
"Breakfast was at seven. The guests were served
tea and coffee and meat, both cold and boiled."

"And did Washington eat the same breakfast?"

The guard looked confused. "I don't know," he
said. "I've only been here eight months."

George and his father and mother went home. They found George's grandmother and Miss Willing waiting together on the front porch.

"No luck," George reported.

Mr. Allen put his hand on George's shoulder. "It was a good try, son," he said. "You can't win them all."

"Sometimes there's nothing to do but give up," Mrs. Allen said.

George's grandmother said she guessed in the long run it didn't matter so much what George Washington ate.

George Allen looked at his family in amazement. "*Give up!*" he shouted. "You expect me to give up! George Washington's soldiers were starving, and they didn't give up. They were freezing, and they didn't give up. *What do you think I am?*"

George was so mad he slammed the screen door and went up to his room. But even upstairs he could hear them talking to Miss Willing about him. George stamped up to the attic. He sat down on the top step. It was quiet here. And very neat. He could see his grandmother had been working.

Next to him was a box filled with things he guessed his grandmother meant to throw away. On top of the box was an old stuffed dog. He remembered that dog. His name was Ginger. One ear was torn now, and the tail was hanging by a thread. Still, he was a good dog. George put him aside.

He looked back in the box. There was a bunch of old Batman comics. It was a good thing he'd come up here, he thought. No one should throw away old comics.

Under the comics George found a book. It was an old book, torn and beat-up-looking—probably his grandfather's, he thought, and it seemed a shame to throw it away. *The American Oracle*, the book was called, and it was written by the Honorable Samuel Stearns, whoever that was.

George whistled as he turned the pages. This honorable Samuel Stearns thought he knew *everything*. He told you how to choose a wife, how to kill bedbugs and how to keep from getting bald. He named the birds of North America (140), and he listed all the famous earthquakes since the year 17 (63 earthquakes). Then there was a chapter called "The Character of Washington."

George looked back at the title page, where he knew he would find the date that the book was published.

"1791," he read. Samuel Stearns was living at the same time as Washington.

George turned back to the chapter on Washington. "Well, Mr. Stearns," George said, "if you know so much, kindly inform me about Washington's breakfast."

"Washington," Mr. Stearns wrote, "raised 7,000 bushels of wheat and 10,000 bushels of corn in one year."

"Okay, okay," George said. "That wasn't the question."

"Washington," Mr. Stearns continued, "is very regular, temperate, and industrious; rises winter and summer at dawn of day."

"Then what?" George asked.

"He breakfasts about seven," Mr. Stearns wrote, "on—"

Suddenly George let out a whoop. He put the book behind his back and clattered down the steps.

"Grandma!" he shouted. "When did you say you'd cook me George Washington's breakfast?"

"Boy, if you ever find out about that breakfast, I'll cook it right then no matter what time it is."

"Right this minute, for instance?"

"That's what I said."

George grinned. He brought the book out from behind his back.

"Washington," he read, "breakfasts about seven o'clock on three small Indian hoecakes and as many dishes of tea."

George passed the book around, and he thought he'd never seen people act as happy. All but his grandmother.

"George," she said, "I don't have the slightest idea what an Indian hoecake is."

**236**

George went to the dictionary. He looked under *H*. "Hoecake. A cake of cornmeal and water and salt baked before an open fire or in the ashes, originally on a hoe."

"I've cornmeal and water and salt," she said. "I guess I can make some Indian hoecakes."

George's father built a fire in the fireplace.

George's mother filled the kettle with water for the tea.

George said he'd go down to the basement for a hoe, but his grandmother stopped him. "You don't want me to cook these things on a *hoe*, do you?" she asked.

"That's what the dictionary says."

"The dictionary says *originally*. That means when hoecakes first came out. I expect they'd been around quite a while before Washington's time."

George wasn't sure. He wanted to do it right.

"Did you see a hoe in Washington's kitchen?"

George admitted there was no hoe there.

"All right then," his grandmother said. "Did you see any black iron griddles?"

George said that he had.

"That's what we'll use," his grandmother said. She mixed cornmeal and water in a bowl; she added salt; then she shaped the mixture in her hands to form little cakes.

Everyone sat around the fire to wait for breakfast. Pretty soon the tea kettle began to steam and the hoecakes began to turn a nice golden brown.

Then George's grandmother served George Washington's breakfast.

George took a bite of hoecake. It was pretty good, he thought. He looked at his mother and his father and his grandmother and Miss Willing all eating hoecakes together on a Sunday afternoon. George decided he felt more related to Washington than he'd ever felt in his whole life. It was as if George Washington were right there at the fireplace with them.

There was only one trouble.

When George finished his three small hoecakes and his three cups of tea, he was still hungry. And if he was hungry, he thought, what about Washington? For a man who was six feet tall and the Father of His Country, it seemed like a skimpy breakfast.

"I hope Washington didn't have long to wait until lunch," he said. "I hope he had a nice big lunch to look forward to. A nice big one. I wonder what—"

But George never finished his sentence. His grandmother was standing up.

"George Washington Allen," she cried. "Don't you *dare!*" And she pointed her spatula at him.

"Not today," Miss Willing said. "The library is closed today."

"Okay." George grinned. "Not today."

## A Reader Says

*I think it was fun to solve the mystery of George Washington's breakfast, but I wouldn't have really eaten it. Hoecakes don't sound too good to me.*

How did you feel about the story?

# About the Author

## Jean Fritz

Jean Fritz was born in China and grew up there. Now she lives in New York State. She likes writing stories about people from America's past.

She has written stories about famous people from American history, including Christopher Columbus, Pocahontas, Patrick Henry, Paul Revere, George Washington, and Benjamin Franklin. She has written over forty books for children and has won many awards for these books.

In *Homesick: My Own Story*, Fritz wrote about growing up in China. The book won an American Book Award. Later she went back to China for a visit. She wrote a book telling about her trip. She loves both the United States and China very much.

Most of all, Fritz loves writing children's books about the life stories of famous Americans. She hopes that children who read about these people will enjoy her books. She believes that they will also find out what made America a great country.

# More Books About Mysteries

**Commander Toad and the Space Pirates**

*by Jane Yolen*

Commander Toad steers his spaceship, *Star Warts*, through outer space in search of adventure. What will he and his faithful frog crew meet up with this time?

**Fantastic Mr. Fox**

*by Roald Dahl*

Mr. Fox just wants to feed his family, but three mean farmers will do anything to stop him. Can Mr. Fox save himself and the other animals of the forest?

**How to Be a Nature Detective**

*by Millicent E. Selsam*

Would you like to solve more mysteries of nature? This book tells you how to explore the world around you.

**Mystery of the Disappearing Dogs**

*by Barbara Brenner*

Why would anyone want to steal a little dog? When their favorite pet disappears, Elena and Michael Garcia decide that they will solve the mystery themselves.

# MAKING ALL THE
# CONNECTIONS

## Speaking and Listening

In this part of the book you read about many kinds of mysteries. Some of these stories were true. Others told about imaginary characters who solved mysteries. You read about the mystery of the neighbor in Apartment 3A. You read about the mystery of why Carruthers was grumpy. You also read about the mysteries of electricity and of George Washington's breakfast. All of these stories made us curious for the answer to an unexplained happening.

Discuss the stories and articles you read with your classmates. You may want to look at your Reader's Log. Speak clearly when you give your ideas. Listen carefully as others share their ideas with you. Here are some questions to help you talk about the unit.

1. How were the mysteries you read about alike or different? Compare how they were solved.
2. Think about your own life. What mysteries have made you curious? Have you solved any of them?
3. Talk about what makes up a mystery. See how many mystery ideas you can think of.

# Reading About a Mystery Strip

In this unit, you have read about mysteries. Now you are going to make a mystery of your own. You are going to make a mystery strip. This poem will tell you a little about it.

A mystery strip is one-sided.
   And you'll get quite a laugh
   If you cut it in half,
For it stays in one piece when divided.

Are you curious? Well, here are some clues.
   A piece of paper has two sides, right? If you draw a line on one side, you have to turn it over to draw a line on the other side, right? Wrong! This is one of the mysteries about the strip that you are going to make.

When you cut a piece of paper in half, you should have two parts, right? Wrong! That is another mystery about the strip that you are going to make.

Are you even more curious? Well, that is how a mystery is supposed to make you feel.

To solve this mystery, you will need a long piece of paper, scissors, glue, and a pencil. Ask your teacher for these things. Then turn the page.

**MAKING ALL THE CONNECTIONS**

# Making a Mystery Strip

Work with a classmate. Use these directions and the pictures to make your own mystery strips.

**1.** Cut out a long strip of paper.

**2.** Write AB on both ends.

AB                                                                                                            AB

**3.** Give the paper a half twist. Your paper should look like this.

AB

**4.** Glue the ends together. Your mystery strip should look like this.

**Step 4**

**5.** Now draw a line down the middle of the strip you have made. Keep going until you come back to the place where you started. What do you notice? Your line is on both sides of the paper and you never turned the paper over!

**Step 5**

**6.** Take your scissors and cut the strip in half, right down the line you drew. When you cut something in half, you should have two parts. What do you have on your mystery strip? It should have two strips twisted together.

**Step 6**

# More Tricks With a Mystery Strip

Here is something else you can try with a mystery strip. Follow these directions.

**1.** Make another mystery strip.

**2.** Draw a line down the middle.

**3.** Draw another line between the middle and the edge of the paper.

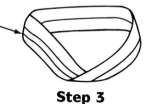

**Step 3**

**4.** Cut the strip right down the new line.

**5.** You should have two rings twisted together!

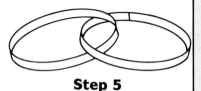

**Step 5**

Do you notice that the smaller strip is another mystery strip? If your paper is wide enough, you can keep cutting the same way. You will have lots and lots of rings! Try it with a new and wider mystery strip.

## Presenting Your Mystery Strip

You can share your Mystery Strip in these ways.
**Color Your Mystery Strip**   Decide with your classmates on four colors to use. Also decide whether you want to make rings or twisted strips. Then color your strips and hang them on the bulletin board.
**Give a Magic Show**   Use a mystery strip to give a magic show.

# PART FOUR

# Ventures

When I stamp
The ground thunders,
When I shout
The world rings,
When I sing
The air wonders
How I do such things.

*At the Top of the World*
by Felice Holman

◆

A venture is something new that may seem
difficult. The people you'll meet in these stories
have had to put their fears aside as they try
something new. As you read, think: Have you ever
tried to do something you weren't sure would
succeed? What new ventures will you try now?

**247**

# Exploring Words About Ventures

## Starting with What You Know

Ventures mean trying something new. When you think of ventures, what ideas come to mind? The words in the box below tell about ventures. Use these words and words of your own to answer the questions after the box.

| | | |
|---|---|---|
| experiment | brave | challenging |
| exciting | new | struggle for |
| able | difficult | take risks |

Some people might say that ventures are challenging. How would you describe a venture? Some people who venture are brave. How would you describe a person who ventures? Some people take risks when they undertake something new. What else might people do when they undertake something new?

## Building a Word Map

The word map shows how some of the words in the box go together. Think about words you can add to the map. Use words from the box and other words of your own.

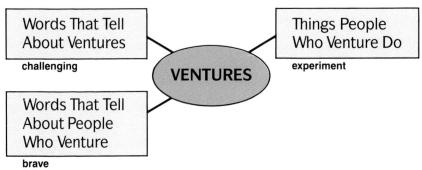

Words That Tell About Ventures
challenging

Things People Who Venture Do
experiment

VENTURES

Words That Tell About People Who Venture
brave

**248**

## Finishing a Story

Look at the story below. The story tells about a girl named Helen who undertakes a venture without even leaving home. Some words are missing. Copy the story on a separate sheet of paper. Use the words from the box and word map in this lesson for ideas. Complete the story.

Helen was tired of her breakfast cereal. She decided to _____. She would make a new cereal for kids. It was a very _____ venture, and one that was _____ too.

Helen was a _____ girl. She went to the store and bought raisins, _____, cereal, and _____. She mixed these things together. Her new cereal was ready. Helen was _____.

She took a bite of her cereal. "This cereal is _____," she said.

Share your story with your class. How were the stories different? What words did your classmates use?

## As You Read

In this part of the book, you will read about ventures and the people who undertake them. Keeping a Reader's Log will help you remember important thoughts, ideas, and words. As you read, make notes in your log. You could begin your Reader's Log with the word map. Add new words to the map as you find them.

Leaving home can be a risky venture. Even though his parents warn him of dangers on the way, the mouse in this story decides to go to the seashore.

# The Mouse at the Seashore

◆

### by Arnold Lobel

A Mouse told his parents that he was going on a trip to the seashore.

"We are very alarmed!" they cried. "The world is full of terrors. You must not go!"

"I have decided to go," said the Mouse firmly. "I have never seen the ocean, and it is high time that I did. Nothing can make me change my mind."

"Then we cannot stop you," said Mother and Father Mouse, "but do be careful!"

The next day, in the first light of dawn, the Mouse began his venture. Even before the morning had ended, the Mouse came to know trouble and fear.

A Cat appeared out from behind a tree.

"I will eat you for lunch," he said.

It was a narrow escape for the Mouse. He ran for his life, but he left a part of his tail in the mouth of the Cat.

By afternoon the Mouse had been attacked by birds and dogs. He had lost his way several times. He was bruised and bloodied. He was tired and frightened.

At evening the Mouse slowly climbed the last hill and saw the seashore spreading out before him. He watched the waves rolling onto the beach, one after another. All the colors of the sunset filled the sky.

"How beautiful!" cried the Mouse. "I wish that Mother and Father were here to see this with me."

The moon and the stars began to appear over the ocean. The Mouse sat silently on the top of the hill. He was overwhelmed by a feeling of deep peace and contentment.

*All the miles of a hard road are worth a moment of true happiness.*

## Thinking About the Theme

**1.** Do you agree with the author that everything that happened to the mouse on the way was worth the happiness he felt at the seashore?

**2.** The mouse wished that his parents were with him at the seashore. Do you think his trip would have been easier if all three of them had gone?

COMPREHENSION
◄BUILDER►

for **Byline: Nellie
Bly** and **Art of
the North
American Indians**

# Understanding
# Main Idea and Details

## Starting with What You Know

What sentence can you make up that says what
the picture is all about?

## Thinking About Main Idea and Details

A **topic** is what a story or paragraph is about. A
topic might be something like "transportation" or
"grasshoppers." A **main idea** is a sentence that
gives the most important idea about the topic. A
main idea might be, "Grasshoppers are interesting
insects." **Details** tell more about the main idea.
Details might tell what makes grasshoppers
interesting. Read the paragraph at the top of the
next page. Name the topic, and tell which sentence
gives the main idea. Then tell what information the
details give.

People today can use many different kinds of transportation. Jet airplanes take people over long distances in a short time. Large boats take people across oceans, but not as fast as do airplanes. People travel on land by train, bus, and car.

The topic of the paragraph is "transportation." The first sentence gives the main idea. The other sentences tell what kinds of transportation people use.

## Practice

Read the paragraph and name the topic. Tell which sentence gives the main idea. Then tell what information the details give.

Almost all newspapers have stories on sports. You will find stories about countries and people in different parts of the world. You will find stories about people and cities in the United States. A newspaper has many different kinds of stories.

## As You Read

Knowing the topic, main idea, and details helps you understand what you are reading.
- What is the story about?
- What is the most important idea?
- What other information is there?

Apply what you know about main idea and details as you read the two selections that follow. Use the side notes to help you.

Years ago, there were many things that women didn't do. But that didn't stop Nellie Bly. She even ventured to try things no one, not even men, had done before.

# BYLINE:
# NELLIE BLY

by Jeanette Cook

For many years most women worked only at home. Their job was to cook food and clean house and take care of children. But in the late 1800s, a few women started looking for work outside the home. This made many people angry.

This article takes place in the past, in the 1800s.

One day a Pittsburgh newspaper had a story that said that a woman should work only at home. Many people who read the story wrote letters to the editor. Most of them agreed with the story.

But one well-written letter did not agree with the story. It said that because America did not use the minds of its women, it was not as strong as it could be. The name at the end of the letter was E. Cochrane.

The editor thought the letter was very good. It had given him something to think about. In a newspaper story, he asked E. Cochrane to come and talk to him about a job. To his surprise, it was not a man, but a young woman, who came to see him. She said that her name was E. Cochrane . . . Elizabeth Cochrane.

Elizabeth needed a job. She had to make a living for herself and her mother. Her family thought that she should be a nurse or a teacher. But Elizabeth wanted to be a reporter.

The main idea is that Elizabeth needed a job. The details tell how she got one.

There had never been a woman reporter at that newspaper. At first the editor was against the idea. He tried to say no to Elizabeth. But after he heard her ideas for stories, he said that he would give her a chance.

Elizabeth began to write exciting stories. On each story she put the name Nellie Bly. This name soon became hers.

Women reporters for other newspapers wrote stories about flowers and dresses. But not Nellie. She wanted to help poor people. She sometimes went to dangerous places to get the stories she wanted.

These details help you understand that Nellie was an unusual person.

At first many readers were upset. They thought it was not right for a young woman to go to such dangerous places. They said it was a man's job to write about a jail or about poor people who had no homes. But more and more people began to read the stories by Nellie Bly.

In the 1800s factories were not safe. When Nellie wrote that factories were dangerous places to work, the owners of the factories became angry. Nellie's editor was worried. He didn't want Nellie to get hurt, so he gave her something less dangerous to do. Nellie began writing about plays and dances.

These stories were easy to write, but Nellie could not forget the poor people who needed her help. At last she left Pittsburgh and began looking for a job as a reporter in New York City.

Many people in New York City had heard of the woman reporter from Pittsburgh, but only one person wanted to give her a job. Joseph Pulitzer was happy to put Nellie to work on his newspaper, the *World*.

Although Nellie's brave ways often upset people, Pulitzer liked her stories. Soon Nellie was again writing stories that helped poor people.

To get her stories, Nellie sometimes pretended to be someone else. She lived with poor people, worked in factories, and even had herself put in jail. This is why readers could believe the things she said in her stories.

The first sentence states the main idea of this paragraph. The details add facts.

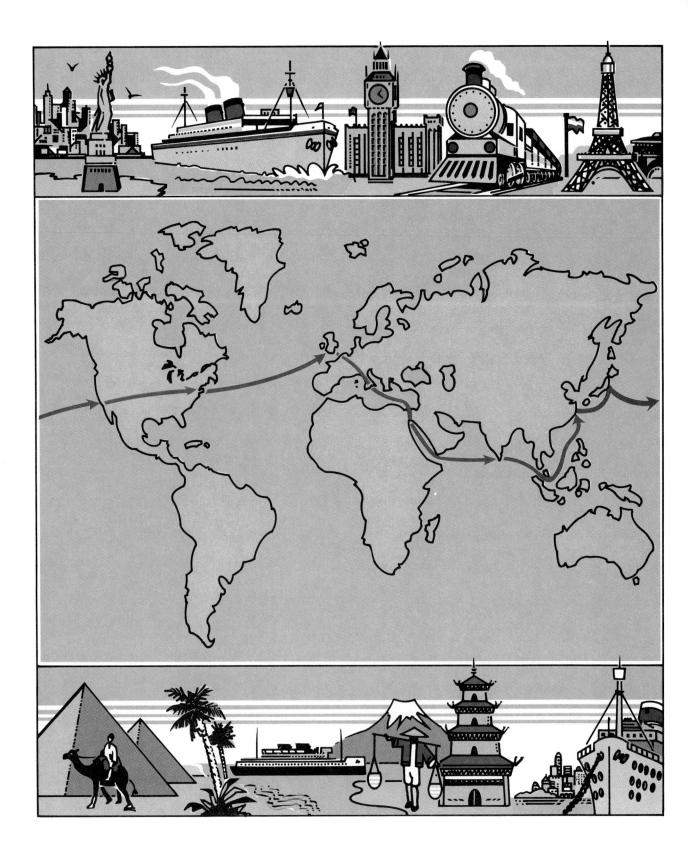

Although Nellie wrote many stories that helped people, she became best known for her trip around the world. She had read Jules Verne's *Around the World in Eighty Days*, a make-believe story about a man's eighty-day trip around the world.

Going around the world in only eighty days sounded impossible, but Nellie thought that it could be done. Joseph Pulitzer agreed with her. He gave her money for the trip.

On November 14, 1889, at 9:40 A.M., Nellie left New Jersey on a steamship. The steamship sailed across the Atlantic Ocean and landed on the south shore of England.

These details describe Nellie's trip.

From England, Nellie sailed to France. Jules Verne came to greet her and wish her luck.   Then she rode in a train to Italy.

Nellie boarded another steamship to travel across the Mediterranean Sea, the Suez Canal, and the Red Sea. Then she went across the Indian Ocean and on to China and Japan.

All along the way she sent back stories about her trip. These stories were used in the *World*. Soon many people had learned of Nellie's race against time. Each day they looked in the *World* for a story by Nellie. Would Nellie make it?

In Japan, Nellie boarded a steamship to cross the Pacific Ocean. When the ship landed in San Francisco, thousands of people were there to greet Nellie. She was filled with joy.

Then Nellie crossed the United States by train. Each time the train stopped, hundreds of people were there to meet her. They had to see Nellie to believe the exciting stories they had read.

On January 26, 1890, at 3:15 P.M., Nellie was back in New Jersey. She had gone around the world faster than any other person. It took her seventy-two days, six hours, and eleven minutes.

And it all started with Elizabeth Cochrane's letter to an editor.

## A Reader Says

*I think the Pittsburgh editor was wrong to keep Nellie from writing the stories she wanted to write. If she wasn't afraid, he shouldn't have been either.*

How did you feel about the article?

# After You Read

## Thinking About What You Read

**1.** Why do you think Nellie Bly challenged the idea that women should work only at home?

**2.** How do you know that Nellie Bly thought differently from other women reporters?

**3.** How do you know Nellie's way of researching news stories was dangerous?

**4.** Why do you think Nellie Bly wanted to prove that a person could go around the world in eighty days?

## Thinking About How You Read

How did understanding main idea and details help you to pick out the most important things that happened to Nellie Bly?

## Sharing and Listening

Do you think Nellie Bly was a brave person? What do you think of her ventures? Share your opinion of Nellie Bly with your classmates. Find facts to support your opinion. Listen as your classmates share their opinions.

## Writing

Suppose you were Nellie Bly and were going around the world. Write a short newspaper article describing an adventure you have had in a foreign country.

**The Indian tribes of North America led lives full of risk and adventure. In this article, you'll see how they expressed their lives through their art.**

# ART OF THE NORTH AMERICAN INDIANS

### by Shirley Petersen

Many beautiful forms of art have come to us from the North American Indians. Much of that art tells a story. The materials the Indians used to tell stories were usually the materials available in the area where they lived.

 **Indians of the Northwest**

In the northwest part of our country, there were many huge trees. So the Indians who lived there made good use of this wood. They made boats, bowls, and cooking utensils from the wood. They also used the wood from the giant red cedar to carve totem poles.

The Northwest Indians used totem poles to tell stories in much the same way people today use pictures in books. The different people in the story, or legend, were carved into the totem pole. Each different figure stood for an important event in the story. The storyteller would "read" the story from top to bottom by telling about the events shown by each figure.

## Indians of the Plains

The Plains Indians also told stories and recorded important events with their art. Unlike the Northwest Indians, they didn't have many trees, but they did have plenty of buffaloes.

The Plains Indians moved around, following the buffalo herds. Buffaloes provided the Plains Indians with meat for food, hides for tepees and clothes, bones for tools, and horns for containers. Nothing was wasted. Men's robes were painted with pictures that recorded brave deeds. Tepees were painted with designs that were supposed to protect the owners from bad times. Each family had its own special design, which could not be copied.

The Plains Indians made their paints with roots, plants, and bark. The paint was put on with a stick or a sharp bone.

Plains Indians were also famous for their beadwork. Beads were used to decorate clothes, moccasins, carrying pouches, and cradles.

 **Indians of the Woodlands**

The Indians who lived on the East Coast and in the midwest part of this country are known as Woodland Indians. Although trees were plentiful, the Woodland Indians used them differently than the Northwest Indians did.

Woodland Indians carved faces on trees, but they didn't make them into totem poles. Instead they used them as masks. These masks were often painted and decorated with feathers. Woodland Indians also made masks from dried corn husks because corn could be grown easily on the land. These masks were used for special ceremonies.

To tell stories or record important events, the Woodland Indians made wampum belts. These were long pieces of cloth with pictures woven into them with wampum beads. Wampum beads were usually made from different kinds of shells.

The Woodland Indians were the first people to use quillwork. The quills of porcupines were dropped into boiling dyes made from berries. Then they were woven together to form a design, or they were stitched directly into the cloth. Quillwork spread to other American Indian groups. It soon became a fine art used to create many beautiful designs.

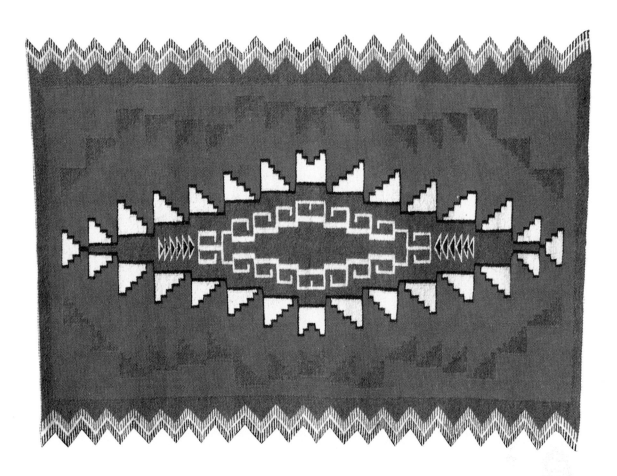

 **Indians of the Southwest**

The Southwest Indians did not have the trees or the buffaloes that other American Indian groups had. But they did have lots of grazing land and clay.

The Southwest Indians became famous for their woven blankets and rugs. They raised goats and sheep for their wool. They made yarn from this wool and dyed it different colors. The yarn was woven on large looms to create blankets and rugs with beautiful designs.

Pottery making was another important art of the Southwest Indians. They cut out a round clay bottom and then rolled clay into snakelike shapes called coils. The coils were then stacked one on top of another until the proper size and shape were reached. Sometimes the Indian potters left the coils as they were. Other times, they smoothed them out and carved or painted designs on them. Pottery for special ceremonies was sometimes shaped into animal figures.

Today, many different kinds of North American Indian art can be found in museums. Many people collect Indian art, also. Many American Indian groups still make these forms of art so that the art of their people will be remembered.

## A Reader Says

*I'd like to make art from things I can find around me, like the Indians did.*

How did you feel about the article?

# After You Read

## Thinking About What You Read

**1.** Why do you think Northwest Indians used totem poles to tell their stories?

**2.** Why do you think the things the North American Indians made were both beautiful and practical?

**3.** Why do you think some North American Indians made their art out of wood, while others used porcupine quills and wool to make art?

**4.** How do you know art was important to the Indians of North America?

## Thinking About How You Read

How did understanding about main idea and details help you find important ideas in this article?

## Sharing and Listening

The Indian tribes of North America decorated their pottery, teepees, robes, and other items with art. Think about how we use art to decorate our homes and the things we wear. Discuss with your classmates the kinds of decorations that you like and why people in all times and places have decorated their homes and clothing. Listen as others give their ideas.

## Writing

Draw a picture of a totem pole. The totem pole can tell a story about life and customs from America's past, or it could tell a story of one of your experiences. Use the totem pole to write a story.

for **Shingebis and the North Wind** and **Stone Soup**

# Understanding Folk Tales

## Starting with What You Know

You have heard or read stories that were made up long, long ago. Some of the stories tell about animals that behave like people. Some of these stories tell about kings or princesses or ordinary people who do something brave or unusual. What stories like these have you heard or read?

## Thinking About Folk Tales

The kind of stories you just talked about are **folk tales.** Folk tales have the same parts that other stories have:

Characters: These are the people or animals in the story.

Setting: This is the place and time when the story happens.

Plot: These are the important events in the story. In some stories, three or more important events make up the plot.

Outcome: This is the way the story ends. In many stories, the main character solves a problem.

Some folk tales teach a lesson about how people should behave. Other folk tales are made-up stories about how something came to be, such as how the elephant got its trunk. Still other folk tales tell about brave deeds.

## Before You Read

Look at the name of the story and look at the pictures. Try to guess what will happen in the story.

## As You Read

Stop after every page. Think about what you have read so far. Try to guess what will happen next. Ask yourself these questions as you read. The questions with blue diamonds are for any kind of story. The questions with red diamonds are for folk tales.

Characters: ◆ Who are the characters?

◆ Do the characters do things that real people can't do?

Setting: ◆ Where and when does the story happen?

◆ Does the story happen long, long ago?

Plot: ◆ What are the important actions?

◆ Do I learn how something came to be?

Outcome: ◆ How does the story end?

◆ What lesson was taught or what brave deed was done?

Apply what you know about reading folk tales as you read the two folk tales that follow. Use the side notes to help you.

Shingebis wants to stay north for the winter, but the rest of his tribe is afraid to risk it. If no one will venture to stay with him, he'll have to face the North Wind alone.

# SHINGEBIS AND THE NORTH WIND

---

a Chippewa Indian folk tale, retold by Sibyl Hancock

---

The story takes place in the north, long ago.

Shingebis is the main character. He is not going with the others.

Fall was almost over, and all the Chippewa were getting themselves ready to travel south for the winter. All except one, that is.

"I'm not leaving!" young Shingebis exclaimed, looking very determined.

"But you must come with us," the Indians shouted, "because soon, when North Wind sweeps over the land, there will be no more fishing, and you will freeze!"

Shingebis shook his head, meaning this year he wouldn't flee to the warm south.

**274**

The Indians murmured among themselves. They agreed that Shingebis was brave, but to face North Wind was frightening.

"You'll be sorry," they said, "because all of your tricks will not help you this time."

"I will not leave," Shingebis replied in a very determined voice.

"North Wind is very strong," the Indians said, "and he uses his strength to blow the huge trees down before him."

Shingebis said, "I'm not worried, because during the day my leather clothes will keep me warm and at night I'll stay by the fire inside my tepee. North Wind won't dare to come inside!"

Here you find out what Shingebis is like.

Think about what might happen to Shingebis.

While everyone else got themselves ready to go, loading their canoes with the fish they had caught, Shingebis laughed and murmured to himself, "I'll show them that they shouldn't have to leave."

When the canoes were out of sight, Shingebis went to work. He tightened his tepee close to the ground, and began drying logs before the fire.

In the evening Shingebis sang before the fire and tried not to be lonely. Each morning he went to the hole he'd cut in the frozen lake, and he caught many fish.

Cold days came, and North Wind howled. He drove all the little animals into their winter homes, he danced in the snowflakes, and trees moaned under his icy touch.

"Woo-oo-oo!" North Wind roared when he found Shingebis. "Who would dare to stay here long after the geese have flown? Who would dare to fight against my strength? Who thinks I am a gentle breeze?"

Great North Wind howled and stirred up cold, icy wind and made the snow drift so high that no creature would dare to travel about—except Shingebis. The young brave stepped right outside his tepee and went fishing.

North Wind said, "I'll freeze his fishing hole, and then Shingebis cannot eat!"

So North Wind roared and blew until the lake was covered with snow and the hole was frozen over.

The wind talks. Ask yourself if this could really happen.

**276**

Determined, Shingebis did not give up, but moved on to another lake, cut a hole, and caught more fish.

"Shingebis must understand my strength!" North Wind howled.

However, each day Shingebis left his tepee to catch more fish, and each day the fierce North Wind couldn't stop him.

"Woo-oo-oo!" North Wind roared, "I'll blow down his door, then Shingebis will surely freeze!"

North Wind howled and roared outside the little tepee, but Shingebis just tossed more logs on his fire, and the wind's icy breath did not make him cold.

"You cannot beat me!" Shingebis shouted.

"I'll cause trouble until you freeze!" North Wind howled, and he slipped under the flap of the tepee.

Guess who will win this battle — Shingebis or the North Wind.

Shingebis shivered, but he didn't say a word when the fierce North Wind sat beside him.

"I will freeze you!" North Wind howled, and he breathed his cold breath. Shingebis didn't look at the terrible North Wind as he reached forward to stir his fire. The fire leaped high, and its shadow played on the wall.

Suddenly North Wind's icy hair began to drip, then his face began to drip, and then his icy clothes began to drip. Fierce North Wind was melting!

Frightened North Wind howled, ran outside, and threw himself into a snowdrift.

"What a strange young man is this Shingebis!" he murmured weakly. "I cannot starve him or freeze him; I haven't even frightened him! I think I shall leave him alone!"

North Wind didn't try to freeze Shingebis anymore. Sunny days came, and Shingebis watched as green buds appeared on trees and grass peeped through the melting snow. He no longer had to fish in a frozen lake, because the ice was melting.

Everyone else came back in their canoes at the first sign of spring. The surprised people were proud of Shingebis because he'd stopped the North Wind and had brought an early spring.

Shingebis did a brave thing. That is why the Chipppewa people told his story over and over again.

## A Reader Says

*I bet Shingebis was glad when the others came back early. He was probably lonely.*

How did you feel about the story?

# After You Read

## Thinking About What You Read

**1.** Why do you think Shingebis was determined to spend the winter in the north?

**2.** Why do you think the North Wind was so determined to make Shingebis sorry he had stayed?

**3.** How do you know that Shingebis was a brave young man?

**4.** How do you know the North Wind was surprised that he was unable to make Shingebis move?

## Thinking About How You Read

How did understanding folk tales help you to figure out the kind of things that Shingebis and the North Wind might do in this story?

## Sharing and Listening

Think about Shingebis and his venture of staying the winter in the north. Do you think he was foolish or brave? Share your opinion with your classmates. Give reasons to support your opinion. Listen to the opinions of your classmates.

## Writing

Imagine that you were Shingebis. Write an entry in your diary describing one of your experiences with the North Wind.

# A Song of Greatness

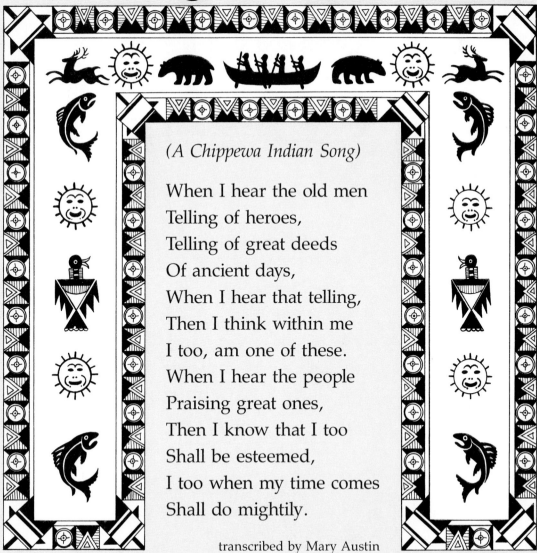

*(A Chippewa Indian Song)*

When I hear the old men
Telling of heroes,
Telling of great deeds
Of ancient days,
When I hear that telling,
Then I think within me
I too, am one of these.
When I hear the people
Praising great ones,
Then I know that I too
Shall be esteemed,
I too when my time comes
Shall do mightily.

transcribed by Mary Austin

A hungry stranger arrives in a town where the people won't even venture out to greet him. But he has an idea that will make them happy to help.

# Stone Soup

by Donna Gruver

## CAST

| | |
|---|---|
| A STRANGER with a beard | MOLLY |
| | JENNY |
| ALICE | VILLAGERS |
| LIZZIE | ELLEN |

**TIME:** *many years ago*

**PLACE:** Lizzie's, Jenny's, *and* Ellen's *houses in a small village. They are working in their houses and they can be seen through large windows. A creek is at right.*

**STRANGER:** *(comes in, holding a kettle and a bag; puts kettle and bag down by feet; speaks to himself)* There is very little daylight left. *(looks at windows)* Maybe these villagers will share some food with me tonight. *(He stands on* Lizzie's *steps to knock on her door.)*

**LIZZIE:** *(turning to window)* Who is it?

**STRANGER:** A wandering stranger. Can you share some food with me tonight?

**LIZZIE:** A wandering stranger, and you ask me for food? No, you can have nothing here! *(goes away from window while* Stranger *stands on* Jenny's *steps to knock on her door)*

**STRANGER:** Hello in there!

**JENNY:** *(turning to window)* What do you want?

**STRANGER:** Some food, please, for a stranger in your village.

**JENNY:** I can't give you any food. I'm saving my food for winter. *(goes away from window)*

**STRANGER:** *(speaking to himself)* I'll go ahead and see if my luck is any better here. *(stands on* Ellen's *steps to knock on her door)*

**ELLEN:** *(turning to window)* Who are you, and why are you here? Daylight is just about over!

**STRANGER:** I'm a wandering stranger, good woman. Please share your dinner with me tonight.

**ELLEN:** If I share my dinner with you, I won't have enough for myself, so go away! (*goes away from window*)

**STRANGER:** (*speaking to himself*) People are supposed to share what they have. There is just enough daylight left, so I'll show them how to make stone soup! (Ellen *comes back to window as he laughs out loud.*)

**ELLEN:** You aren't supposed to stay here, Stranger, so go ahead and leave our village!

**STRANGER:** (*pretends not to hear*) I will start a fire here. (*finds sticks and throws them down at his feet; pretends to start a fire with sticks*) I wonder if they have good stones here. (*puts kettle by creek and throws some stones into it as* Lizzie *and* Jenny *look at him from their windows*)

**STRANGER:** What kinds of stones are these? (*As he puts kettle by sticks,* Lizzie, Jenny, *and* Ellen *leave houses and come near fire.* Alice, Molly, *and other* Villagers *come in and whisper to each other as* Ellen *stands close to the* Stranger.)

**ELLEN:** What are you going to cook?

**STRANGER:** Just some stone soup. You can help me choose the stones.

**ELLEN:** I never heard of stone soup.

**STRANGER:** (*pretends to be surprised*) I don't believe it! Well, help me choose some good stones and you may share mine. (*He looks into kettle.*) I'm saving this big one because it came from a mountain and it will taste like snow. I'll throw that one away . . . a flat stone, a flat taste! (Villagers *whisper to each other as he throws flat stone away.*) We're supposed to use the best! Now I'll get some water. (*puts kettle on fire and puts in water from the creek as* Villagers *whisper to each other again*) Who has a spoon to taste the soup?

**ELLEN:** I have a nice big spoon that I've been saving for a party.

**STRANGER:**  Good! (Ellen *goes into her house to get spoon*.)

**ALICE:**  (*speaking to* Molly) Who is the stranger with the beard? Did he say he can make soup from stones?

**MOLLY:**  Yes, I saw him put some in the kettle.

**LIZZIE:**  I'm getting hungry! (Ellen *comes out and gives spoon to the* Stranger, *who smiles at her.*)

**STRANGER:**  Thank you. (*stirs and tastes*)

**MOLLY:**  I'm starving! (*sniffs*) It must be the smell of the soup.

**ALICE:**  (*sniffs*) I must have a terrible cold, because I can't smell it.

**MOLLY:**  (*sniffs*) How good it smells! (*The* Stranger *stirs, tastes, and smiles.*)

**STRANGER:**  It's delicious.

**ELLEN:**  I'm starving, too, so let me taste it! (*She tries to take the spoon and he pretends not to see her.*)

**STRANGER:** It's supposed to have some celery and
onions in it.

**JENNY:** I have some celery and onions.

**VILLAGERS:** Hurry, Jenny! We are starving! Go
ahead and get them! (Jenny *goes into the
house.*)

**STRANGER:** (*tastes soup*) And it's really supposed to
have some carrots.

**LIZZIE:** I'll get some carrots.

**STRANGER:** Thank you. You're invited to be my
guest. (Lizzie *goes into house, and* Jenny
*comes out and gives bag to the* Stranger.)

JENNY: Use all you need.

STRANGER: Thank you for the celery and onions. You will be my guest, won't you? (*The* Stranger *puts some celery and onions in, and then he tastes soup again.*) Some potatoes would make it really delicious. (Lizzie *comes back with the carrots, and the* Stranger *puts them in.*)

MOLLY: (*speaking to* Villagers) I want to be invited, too! (*They all whisper as* Molly *leaves, then comes back with a bag and gives it to the* Stranger.)

STRANGER: Thank you. You're invited to be my guest, too. (*He puts potatoes in.*) Oh, no, this is terrible! I put too many potatoes in, and they will cover up the taste of the stones!

VILLAGERS: No! How terrible!

ELLEN: Let's put in some ham. I will get some. (*She goes in.*)

STRANGER: That might work—and bring some bowls and spoons! (Ellen *comes back with ham, bowls, and spoons. The* Stranger *puts the ham in, and then he stirs and tastes.*)

ALICE: How is it now? It smells delicious.

STRANGER: It needs some salt and pepper. (Jenny *goes into house and comes back with salt and pepper. The* Stranger *puts salt and pepper in, and he tastes again. He stirs the soup thoughtfully. The* Villagers' *excitement grows.*)

**STRANGER:** The stone soup is ready to eat, all of you! (*The* Villagers *take bowls to the* Stranger *for soup and they all eat.*)

**EVERYONE:** M-m-m-m! Delicious!

**ELLEN:** And just think of it . . . it's made only of stones! (*The Stranger smiles.*)

**STRANGER:** Yes, it's made only of stones!

## A Reader Says

*I think people will find out what the Stranger did when they try to make stone soup again. They'll probably be angry with him.*

How did you feel about the play?

# After You Read

## Thinking About What You Read

1. Why do you think Lizzie and Ellen were both unwilling to share food with the stranger?
2. How do you know that the stranger is a very clever man?
3. Why do you think the villagers never thought to share what they had in the first place?
4. Do you think the villagers learned an important lesson from the stranger? Why or why not?

## Thinking About How You Read

How did knowing about folk tales help you to understand the people and events in this play?

## Sharing and Listening

Sometimes a difficult problem can change people. What problem do you think the villagers faced? Do you think the villagers were cruel for not sharing their food with the stranger? Why or why not? Share your opinion with your classmates. Give reasons to support your opinion. Listen to the opinions of your classmates.

## Writing

Write down the recipe for stone soup. Include all the ingredients, as well as the directions for making the soup.

Obadiah doesn't think that Rachel can do anything as well as he. Rachel thinks she can prove him wrong.

# Rachel and Obadiah

by Brinton Turkle

294

It was a warm, sunny day on Nantucket Island.
No one was stirring on India Street. But back of the
old Pinkham house, Rachel and Obadiah Starbuck
were busy picking blackberries.

Rachel's pail was almost full. Obadiah's pail was
only half full.

"If thee eats all thy berries," Rachel told her
brother, "Mother won't have enough for a pie."

Obadiah popped another big blackberry into his
mouth. Juice trickled down his chin. "I'm not
eating them all," he said. "Just some."

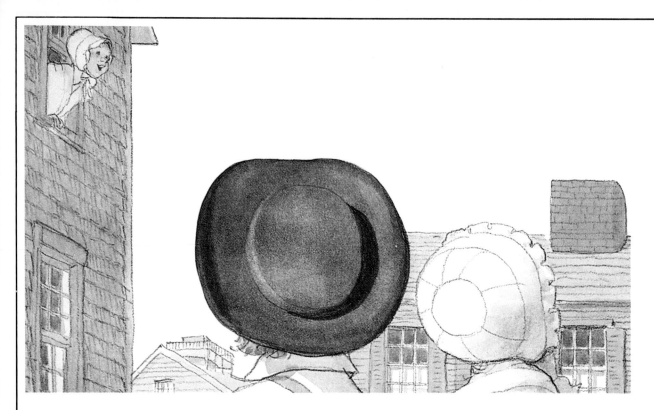

"Elizabeth! Elizabeth Woods!" Across the alley, Jessamy Morse was leaning out of her window, calling to her neighbor.

Elizabeth Woods raised her window and poked her head out.

"Has thee heard?" cried Jessamy Morse. "It's the *Clio*. She's at the bar! A boy brought Sarah Coffin the news. All well on board! Nathaniel is home safe; so is Abraham and thy Jabez, too. All safe!"

"Praise God!" said Elizabeth Woods. "I'll get the baby and see thee at the wharf."

Both windows banged shut.

Suddenly, all Nantucket was astir. The *Clio* had been to sea for more than a year. Everyone seemed to be running to greet her.

Rachel and Obadiah ran, too. They wiggled right up to the edge of the dock to watch the ship—her flags waving and sails billowing—come home.

Asa was showing something to his friends. "What's that?" Obadiah asked his brother.

Asa held up a silver coin. "From the captain's wife," he said. "I was going by Jacob Slade's mill, when he runs up to me and says he's just sighted the *Clio* rounding the bar. He bids me run down to Captain Coffin's house with the news. And Sarah Coffin gives me this!"

Asa let Obadiah hold the money. It was new and very shiny.

Obadiah gave it back. "Does thee think Jacob Slade would ever send me with the news?" he said.

"The *Speedwell*'s due next week," said Asa. "I reckon he might, if thee is at his mill when he sights her."

At suppertime, Mother, Father, Moses, and Rebecca heard all about how Asa earned his prize.

Obadiah said, "Next week, the *Speedwell*'s coming in. I'm going up to the mill every day until Jacob Slade sights her."

"So am I," said Rachel.

"Thee!" Obadiah laughed. "He'd never send thee. Girls can't run. Not as fast as boys."

"We can, too!" said Rachel.

Mother said, "Girls can pick more blackberries than boys."

"I can *too* run fast," said Rachel. "Jacob Slade would send me, wouldn't he, Father?"

Father kissed Rachel. "I know *I* would," he said. "I think Jacob Slade would, too."

The next day was First Day.

The Starbuck family were all at Meeting. So was Jacob Slade. After Meeting, Obadiah went up to him and said, "If I happened to be at thy mill and thee happened to sight a ship, would thee send me to the captain's house with the news?"

"Why, of course, lad. If thee is a good runner."

In a very tiny voice, Rachel said, "Would thee send me?"

"Well now," said the miller. "A girl's never carried the news. But I don't know why not."

"She can't run fast," said Obadiah.

"I can, too!" said Rachel.

Early the next day, Obadiah went right up to the mill. Rachel went right after him.

Jacob Slade scratched his chin. "Thee could have a mighty long wait," he said. "I don't know when the *Speedwell*'s coming in. Could be this week—or next. She might not even come in at all. Besides, how could I send both of you?"

Obadiah said, "We can have a race. We can run down to Pleasant Street, and back up Mill Street to Prospect. Thee could send the winner."

"Does that seem fair, Obadiah?" said the miller. "Rachel is smaller than thee."

"She can start first," said Obadiah.

After a moment, Jacob Slade said, "All right, if Rachel gets a head start."

"Get ready. Get set," said the miller. When he said "Go!" Rachel went.

Soon she was running down Pleasant Street. Someone was on the stoop of Grandmother Mitchell's house. It was Aunt Dorcas with a big basket. "My goodness, Rachel," she said. "Wherever is thee going in such a hurry?"

"A race," said Rachel. "I'm winning." And she kept on running.

Near Summer Street, Rachel heard footsteps pounding behind her. It was Obadiah. He caught up to her and ran a circle around her, showing off.

But, suddenly, Obadiah let out a whoop and dashed over to a field next to the Bunker house. "Blackberries!" he shouted. "Millions of them! I can pick a bushel and still catch up to thee!"

Rachel kept on running.

Turning into Mill Street, she caught her foot in her petticoat and fell down. Rachel began to cry. Why, oh why couldn't she wear britches like a boy?

A wagon creaked by. "Whoa!" said the driver. "What's the matter, little girl? Are you hurt?"

Rachel picked herself up and wiped her tears away with her fist. "No," she said. And she kept on running.

Ahead was Prospect Street. Behind, Obadiah was nowhere in sight.

Just over the top of the hill, getting nearer and nearer, were the vanes of Jacob Slade's windmill slowly turning.

Rachel kept on running.

Jacob Slade was waiting with a big smile on his face. "Thee's won!" he exclaimed. "Good for thee, Rachel Starbuck!"

Was it true? Had she really won? Where was Obadiah?

The miller said, "Does thee think thee can run any farther?"

Rachel nodded her head. "I can run *much* farther," she said.

Jacob Slade took her by the hand. "Let me show thee something," he said.

"Look yonder. Out by Brant Point."

"A ship!" said Rachel. "Is she . . .?"

"The *Speedwell*!" said the miller. "She's early. See her flags? They show all's well aboard. Does thee think thee can run to Captain Hussey's house with the good news?"

"Yes," said Rachel. "Oh, yes!"

Lydia Hussey wiped her eyes and blew her nose. "I dreamed the *Speedwell* was lost at sea," she said. "Praise the Lord that wasn't true."

The captain's wife gave Rachel a hug, then went to her cupboard and pulled out a brass box from behind a blue teapot. She took a silver coin from the box and gave it to Rachel.

"Thank thee, dear child," she said.

She put on her shawl and bonnet. Then she began to cry all over again. "'All well on board,' did thee say?"

Lydia Hussey got another coin from the box and pressed it into Rachel's hand. "Bless thee, Rachel Starbuck. Thee brings the gladdest tidings."

Rachel got another hug and a rather wet kiss.

Once again, all Nantucket was astir.

Rachel stood at the gate of Captain Hussey's house, looking at the two beautiful pieces of silver. Whatever would she do with two of them?

Down the street came Obadiah. Blackberry juice was all over his face, and he looked very angry.

Rachel put one coin in her pocket. She would
keep it forever.

And she knew just what to do with the other one.

## A Reader Says

*I think Obadiah was lucky to have a sister like Rachel.
She didn't have to share her coins with him, but she did.*

How did you feel about the story?

# About the Author

## Brinton Turkle

Brinton Turkle was born in Ohio and grew up there. He started drawing when he was a child. He says, "I can't remember when I didn't draw."

Mr. Turkle studied drama and art in college. He began drawing pictures for textbooks. Then he visited the island of Nantucket in Massachusetts. The charm of the island stayed with him. Out of his visit grew his first story about Obadiah and Rachel, and life in Nantucket long ago. He has since written many stories about these characters. Two more of these stories are *Thy Friend, Obadiah* and *Obadiah the Bold*.

Mr. Turkle writes in many different ways. He fills his stories with suspense. He also makes them funny. But whatever his stories are like, they all show children that people can be kind and gentle. He hopes his books will play a part in building a better world.

# More Books About Ventures

**Beauty and the Beast**

*by Marianna Mayer*

The Beast is a kind and lonely creature who loves Beauty, a young girl. Can Beauty be brave enough to love him back?

**Bringing the Rain to Kapiti Plain**

*by Verna Aardema*

It hasn't rained on Kapiti Plain for a long time, and the animals are thirsty. Even the grass is turning brown. Ki-pat knows he must do something to make it rain or both his people and the animals of Kapiti Plain will be in serious trouble.

**On the Day Peter Stuyvesant Sailed into Town**

*by Arnold Lobel*

It takes hard work and many years for a tiny village to become a big city like New York. In this book you'll read about the famous man whose skillful leadership gave rise to one of the biggest cities in the world.

**The Story of Ferdinand**

*by Munro Leaf*

A peaceful country bull who loves nothing more than looking at flowers is taken to the city against his will. Once there, he is put in the bull ring to fight. Will he?

# MAKING ALL THE
# CONNECTIONS

## Speaking and Listening

The stories in this part of the book told about ventures both great and small. You read about a mouse who ventured out to the seashore. You read about Nellie Bly, who showed that a woman could venture around the world and write about it for a newspaper. You read about a stranger's venture into a new town and how he cleverly fooled the selfish townsfolk. You also read about how a young boy ventured to face the North Wind alone, and about how Rachel ventured to do everything her brother could do. Discuss these stories with your classmates. Speak clearly and slowly when you give your thoughts. Listen carefully to the thoughts of others. Use these questions to help you.

**1.** The characters in the stories you read all ventured to go to new places and try new things. Compare their ventures.

**2.** Think about the characters in the stories. Whose venture would you have liked to go along on? Explain you reasons.

**3.** Discuss with your classmates why you think that people want to venture to unknown places.

# Reading Something New in Science

*Each spring and fall, many birds venture toward warmer climates. These journeys have interested scientists for hundreds of years. As you read this article, think about why the birds fly away.*

Have you ever seen hundreds of birds flying in the same direction across the sky? What you are looking at is migration. Migration means "to go from one place to another." In the fall, when the weather grows cold, the birds fly to a warmer place. The birds return in the spring.

How do birds find their way? One answer is that birds use the light of the sun and the stars to guide them.

Scientists also know that birds have a good sense of smell. Birds can find their winter homes by following the smell of those places.

How far can birds fly? Scientists have tracked birds by putting bands around their legs. This way, they know where the bird started out when the bird is found again. Sometimes a tiny radio transmitter is attached to the bird. Then the bird can be tracked by radar. One bird flew 1,900 miles in only six days!

Twice a year birds make these long and sometimes dangerous journeys. They do all of this to return to their warm-weather homes.

**MAKING ALL THE CONNECTIONS**

# Thinking About Ventures

The article you just read was like the stories and articles you have read in this part of the book. It is about a venture. Think about the migrating birds. What is their venture? Why did they set out on this venture? What is your opinion of this article? Think about the stories and articles you have read. Ask yourself the same questions that you asked about the venture of the birds. Then write down the sentences below and use what you have read to finish them.

> The birds' venture was _____.
> They set out because _____.
> My opinion of this article is _____.

Look back at the sentences you wrote. Think about the kinds of ventures you have read about. Pick at least one more venture and write three sentences. In the first, tell what the venture was. In the second, tell why the person or animal set out. In the third, tell your opinion of the story or article.

Can you remember a book about a venture that you really enjoyed? Maybe you would like to write about the story. Write three sentences about the book. You can add more than one book and decide later which one you want to write more about.

# Writing a Book Report

Now it is time to write a book report about a venture. Look at the book report in the Handbook at the back of this book. It is a good example of what a book report should look like. Read these steps to help you plan and write your book report.

## Planning

Begin by studying the features of a book report.

- A book report lists the title and the author.
- It lists the main characters.
- It describes the time and place, or setting, of the story.
- It tells the main events, or plot, in the story without giving away the ending.
- It tells why the writer of the book report liked or disliked the book.

Use the chart you filled out to help you select a book to write your report about. If you cannot think of a book, you may wish to write about one of the stories you have read.

## Composing

Now it is time to write your first draft.

- Brainstorm your ideas with a classmate.
- Review your chart for information on the characters, the venture they attempt, the outcome, and your opinion of the story.

**MAKING ALL THE CONNECTIONS**

## Proofreading Marks

∧ add

✗ take out

≋ capitalize

／ lower case

Andy adds these descriptive words to give a clearer picture of the kite.

Andy adds the word *older* to be more exact in his description of Arthur.

## Revising

Now that you have written your first draft, your next step is to revise your writing. The following checklist will help you.

**Revising Checklist**
- ✔ Did I use all the features of a book report?
- ✔ Have I used exact language?
- ✔ Where can I add descriptive language?

Andy has written a first draft of his book report. He is going to revise it. Andy uses the Revising Checklist, and uses proofreading marks to show his corrections.

> Book Title: A Kite For Bennie
> Author: Genevieve Gray
> What Happens? Walking home in his new sneakers, Bennie sees a ∧*high-flying red* kite and decides to make one. His freinds and teachers help. his ∧*older* brother Arthur helps, too. The kite will not fly. I liked the book because of how Bennie made the kite fly

## Proofreading

Now that you have revised your first draft, your next step is to revise punctuation and spelling. The following checklist will help you.

**Proofreading Checklist**

✔ Do my sentences begin with capital letters?
✔ Did I put the correct end mark at the end of each sentence?
✔ Did I capitalize the first word and each important word in the title of the book?
✔ Did I underline the title of the book?

Andy looks at his book report again. He checks errors in spelling, punctuation, and capitalization. Andy uses the Proofreading Checklist to help him.

Book Title: <u>A Kite For Bennie</u>
Author: Genevieve Gray
What Happens? Walking home in his new sneakers, Bennie sees a high-flying red kite and decides to make one. His friends and teachers help. his older brother Arthur helps, too. The kite will not fly. I liked the book because of how Bennie made the kite fly.

Andy underlines the title of the book.

Andy fixes a spelling mistake.

Andy begins the sentence with a capital letter.

Andy puts a period at the end of a sentence.

Now it is your turn to revise. Work with a classmate. Use his or her ideas and the checklists when you revise. Make a neat final copy.

## Presenting

You can share your book report with the class in these ways.

**Reading Aloud**   Read your book report to the class. Ask how many want to read this book.

**Presenting a Play**   While you describe the story, have some friends act it out.

This handbook can help you when you write. It gives you proofreading marks to use when changing your writing. It lists grammar and mechanics rules to help you write correctly, and spelling rules to help you check your spelling. It gives information on how to combine sentences to make your writing smoother. You will also find a model to follow when writing a book report.

Use these proofreading marks when you make changes in your writing.

| Marks | | Examples |
|---|---|---|
| ∧ | add | What time *did* the bus leave? |
| ℓ | take away | Jim walked and I walked to the station. |
| ¶ | indent | ¶ I am writing you today. |
| ≡ | capitalize | John smith. |
| / | small letter | William Black |
| ⬭ | check spelling | They left *yesterday* (yesturday). |
| ∫ | transpose | Seeign you was nice. |

# Grammar

## Sentences

The rules below show the different kinds of sentences and how to use them.

| Rules | Examples |
|---|---|
| A **sentence** is a group of words that tells a complete thought. A sentence starts with a capital letter and ends with an end mark. | **The boy is walking the dog.** |
| A **statement** is a sentence that tells something. Put a period at the end of a statement. | A baby dog is called a puppy**.** |
| A **question** is a sentence that asks for information. Put a question mark at the end of a question. | Which team won the game**?** |
| A **command** is a sentence that tells somebody to do something. Put a period at the end of a command. | Put the books over there**.** |
| An **exclamation** is a sentence that shows strong feeling or surprise. Put an exclamation mark at the end of an exclamation. | Look at that beautiful horse**!** |
| The **complete subject** of a sentence tells whom or what the sentence is about. | **The store's owner** is nice. |
| The **complete predicate** of a sentence tells what the subject does. | My friend Joe **is from New York**. |

## Grammar

### Nouns

The rules below explain the different kinds of nouns and how to form their plurals.

| Rules | Examples |
|---|---|
| A **noun** is a word that names a person, place, or thing. | The **man** rode his **horse** across the **field**. |
| A **singular** noun is a word that names one person, place, or thing. | The **girl** will buy one **apple** at the **store**. |
| A **plural** noun is a word that names more than one person, place, or thing. | Those three **students** won **prizes**. |
| Add **es** to form the plural of nouns that end in **s**, **ss**, **sh**, **ch**, or **x**. If a noun ends in a consonant and **y**, change the **y** to **i** and add **es** to form the plural. | class**es**  box**es**<br>bench**es**  dish**es**<br>cherr**y**  cherr**ies** |
| Some nouns do not follow rules. They change their spelling to form the plural. | foot → feet<br>child → children |
| A **common noun** names any person, place, or thing. A common noun begins with a small letter. | The **man** lives in the **city**. |
| A **proper noun** names a particular person, place, or thing. Capitalize the most important words in a proper noun. | **Mary Johnson** lives in **Center City**. |

# Grammar

## Verbs

The rules below tell about the different kinds of verbs and how to use them.

| Rules | Examples |
|---|---|
| An **action verb** is a word that tells what someone or something does. | The girl **fixed** the bike. |
| A verb in the **present tense** tells about an action that happens now. | Juan **looks** at the sky. |
| A verb in the **past tense** tells about an action that already happened. Most past tense verbs end in **ed**. | We **looked** for the ball. |
| The verb **be** is a **linking verb**. A linking verb joins the subject of a sentence with the words that name or describe it. | She **is** a good singer. Her songs **are** pretty. |
| A **main verb** is the most important verb in a sentence. A **helping** verb helps the main verb tell about an action. Add **ed** to most main verbs that follow the helping verbs **have**, **has**, or **had**. | I **have worked** here before. |
| Irregular verbs do not form the past tense by adding **ed**. | The family **ate** dinner. I **went** to the game. |

## Mechanics

### Capital Letters and Commas

The following rules will help you use capital letters and commas correctly.

| Rules | Examples |
|---|---|
| Capitalize each important word in a proper noun, such as people's names and titles, names of months, days of the week, and specific places or things. | **M**r. **J**osé **L**opez<br>**N**ovember<br>**B**edford **S**treet<br>**R**ocky **M**ountains |
| Use a comma to set off the name of a person spoken to directly in a sentence. | John**,** put the books there. |
| Use a comma after **yes**, **no**, and **well** when they begin a sentence. | No**,** I wasn't there. |
| Use a comma after a time order word when it begins a sentence. | First**,** walk two blocks.<br>Then**,** turn left. |
| Use a comma to separate three or more items in a series. | I bought eggs**,** milk**,** and bread. |
| Use a comma before the word **and** when you join two complete thoughts into a compound sentence. | I went to Joe's house**,** and he gave me the books. |

# Apostrophes

The rules below will help you use apostrophes correctly.

| Rules | Examples |
|---|---|
| To make the possessive form of a singular noun or a plural noun that does not end in **s**, add an apostrophe and **s**. | Lani**'s** paintings<br>men**'s** shirts |
| To make the possessive form of most plural nouns, add an apostrophe at the end of the word. | lions**'** dens<br>giraffes**'** necks |

# Abbreviations

The rules below will help you use abbreviations correctly.

| Rules | Examples |
|---|---|
| Capitalize the first letter in abbreviations of proper nouns and addresses. | **D**r. **L**ipper   **M**s. **J**ohnson<br>**M**aple **S**t.   **B**each **A**ve.<br>**F**eb.   **M**on. |
| End most abbreviations with periods. | Mr**.** Brown<br>Aug**.** |
| For an initial in a person's name, use a capital letter followed by a period. | **D. M.** Walker<br>**J.** Lipton |
| To abbreviate ordinal numbers, write a numeral and an ending, but no period. | 1**st**   2**nd**   3**rd**<br>31**st**   25**th**   43**rd** |

## Spelling Strategies

**1.** You can learn to spell a word in three ways. Which way works best for you?

- ◆ Look at the word. See the letters in it. Picture the word in your mind, remembering the order of its letters.
- ◆ Say the word aloud. Hear the sounds in it. What letter or letters make each sound?
- ◆ Write the word. Practice making the letters. You can also write the words you misspell in a notebook. Write the words correctly. Make the notebook like a dictionary by using one page for each letter of the alphabet. Review your words each week.

**2.** Always check your spelling when you proofread. Follow these steps:

- ◆ Circle each word you think is misspelled.
- ◆ Write the word again. Does it look correct?
- ◆ Check in a dictionary if you are not sure.

**3.** Some words share the same letter pattern. By knowing a pattern, you can spell many words.

- ◆ Words with the **-and** pattern include:
  band   hand   land   sand   stand
- ◆ Words with the **-eat** pattern include:
  beat   feat   heat   meat   seat

What other spelling patterns do you know?

# Models

## A Book Report

Use the book report below as a model for writing book reports of your own.

*George Washington's Breakfast* by Jean Fritz is about a young boy, George W. Allen, who wants to solve a very special mystery. George was born on George Washington's birthday and was named after him. George wants to find out everything he can about our first President. He already knows where President Washington lived and how tall he was. But after school one day he decides to find the answer to just one more question—what George Washington ate for breakfast. He looks for the answer in the school library and in his own house. His parents even take him on a weekend trip to Washington, D.C., and Mt. Vernon, where George Washington lived.

This is a well-written book that is informative and often very funny. Because the characters seem like real people, readers will be interested in finding out how George solved his mystery. The book also includes a lot of valuable information about the way President Washington lived.

*The title and author are included, and the main character is named.*

*The main events are described.*

*The setting is described.*

*The writer does not give away the ending.*

*The writer tells why he likes or dislikes the book.*

# Glossary

This Glossary can help you find the meaning and pronunciation of some of the words found in this book. Use it when you are having problems with a particular word. The directions below will help you understand how the Glossary works.

The pronunciation of each word is shown just after the word, in this way: **ab·bre·vi·ate** (ə brē′vē āt).

The letters and signs used are pronounced as in the words in the pronunciation key below.

The mark ′ is placed after a syllable with a primary or heavy accent, as in the example above.

The mark ′ after a syllable shows a secondary or lighter accent, as in **ab·bre·vi·a·tion** (ə brē′vē ā′shən).

## Full Pronunciation Key

| | | | | | |
|---|---|---|---|---|---|
| **a** | hat, cap | **j** | jam, enjoy | **th** | thin, both |
| **ā** | age, face | **k** | kind, seek | **ŦH** | then, smooth |
| **ä** | father, far | **l** | land, coal | | |
| | | **m** | me, am | **u** | cup, butter |
| **b** | bad, rob | **n** | no, in | **u̇** | full, put |
| **ch** | child, much | **ng** | long, bring | **ü** | rule, move |
| **d** | did, red | | | | |
| | | **o** | hot, rock | **v** | very, save |
| **e** | let, best | **ō** | open, go | **w** | will, woman |
| **ē** | equal, be | **ô** | order, all | **y** | young, yet |
| **ėr** | term, learn | **oi** | oil, voice | **z** | zero, breeze |
| | | **ou** | house, out | **zh** | measure, seizure |
| **f** | fat, if | | | | |
| **g** | go, bag | **p** | paper, cup | | a in about |
| **h** | he, how | **r** | run, try | | e in taken |
| | | **s** | say, yes | **ə =** | i in pencil |
| **i** | it, pin | **sh** | she, rush | | o in lemon |
| **ī** | ice, five | **t** | tell, it | | u in circus. |

# A a

**a·board** (ə bôrd′), on board; in or on a ship, train, bus, or airplane: *"All aboard!" shouted the conductor. We had to be aboard the ship by noon.* adverb, preposition.

**a·dore** (ə dôr′), **1** to love and admire very greatly: *She adores her mother.* **2** to like very much: *I just adored that movie.* verb; **a·dored**.

**a·gainst** (ə genst′), **1** not on the same side as: *Our team will play against yours.* **2** upon or toward; in a different direction from: *Rain beat against the window. We sailed against the wind.* preposition.

**a·gree** (ə grē′), **1** to have the same feeling or ideas: *We all agree on that subject. I agree that we should try to be more careful.* **2** to be in harmony; to be the same as: *Your story about what happened agrees with mine.* verb.

**a·head** (ə hed′), **1** in front; before: *Walk ahead of me.* **2** forward: *Go ahead with this work for another week.* adverb.

**al·ley** (al′ē), a narrow street behind or between buildings in a city. noun.

alley

**a·maze·ment** (ə māz′mənt), great surprise; sudden wonder: *I was filled with amazement when I first saw the ocean.* noun.

**an·kle** (ang′kəl), the joint that connects the foot with the leg. noun, plural **an·kles.**

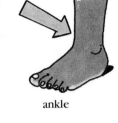
ankle

**anx·ious·ly** (angk′shəs lē), **1** with worry: *Families of people on the missing plane were anxiously waiting for more news.* **2** eagerly: *The children anxiously opened their presents.* adverb.

**ap·pear** (ə pir′), **1** to be seen; come in sight: *One by one the stars appear.* **2** to seem; look: *The apple appeared fresh on the outside, but it was spoiled inside.* verb.

| a hat | ou out | ng long |
|---|---|---|
| ā age | u cup | sh she |
| ä far | u̇ put | th thin |
| e let | ü rule | ŦH then |
| ē equal | ch child | zh measure |
| ėr term | | |
| i it | | |
| ī ice | | ⎰a in about |
| o hot | | e in taken |
| ō open | ə = | ⎱i in pencil |
| ȯ order | | o in lemon |
| oi oil | | u in circus |

**art** (ärt), **1** painting, drawing, and sculpting. **2** a branch of learning that depends more on special practice than on general principles. Writing is an art; botany is a science. The fine arts include painting, drawing, sculpting, architecture, music, and dancing. *noun.*

attic

**at·tic** (at′ik), the space in a house just below the roof and above the other rooms. *noun.* [*Attic* comes from the words *attic story*, meaning "the top story of a building." It was called this because people used to build the top stories of their houses to look like the buildings of Attica, a district of Ancient Greece.]

# B b

**be·come** (bi kum′), **1** to come to be; grow to be: *It becomes colder at night. I became tired and fell asleep.* **2** to look good on; *That blue sweater becomes you. verb.*

**bend** (bend), **1** a part that is not straight; turn: *There is a sharp bend in the road here.* **2** to make or become bent; *bend a wire. The branch began to bend as I climbed along it.* **1** *noun,* **2** *verb.*

**be·tween** (bi twēn′), **1** in the space or time separating two objects or places: *The valley lay between two mountains. We don't go to school between Friday and Monday.* **2** in the range of: *She earned between ten and twelve dollars. preposition.*

**bil·lion** (bil′yən), one thousand millions; 1,000,000,000; a very great amount. *noun, adjective.* **billions**, more than one billion.

biscuit

**bis·cuit** (bis′kit), a soft bread baked in small amounts. *I love to eat fresh biscuits in the morning.* *noun, plural* **bis·cuits.**

**blend** (blend), to mix together; mix or become mixed so thoroughly that the things mixed cannot be told apart or separated: *Blend the butter and the milk before adding the other ingredients of the cake.* *verb,* **blended.**

**bloom** (blüm), to have flowers; open into flowers; blossom: *Many plants bloom in the spring.* *verb,* **bloomed.**

**bod·y** (bod′ē), **1** the whole material part of a person or animal: *I run to keep my body strong and healthy.* *noun.*

bonnet
(def. 1)

**bon·net** (bon′it), **1** a covering for the head often tied under the chin with strings or ribbons, worn by women and children. **2** a headdress of feathers worn by some North American Indians. *noun.*

**bot·tom** (bot′əm), the lowest part: *These berries at the bottom of the basket are crushed.* *noun.*

**brain** (brān), the organ in the head that thinks and learns: *We remember things with our brains.*

**brains** (brānz), ability to learn and know: *A dog has more brains than a worm.* *noun.*

**breathe** (brēŦH), **1** to draw air into the lungs and force it out. You breathe through your nose or through your mouth. **2** to say softly; whisper: *Don't breathe a word of this to anyone.* *verb.*

**build** (bild), to make by putting materials together: *Birds build nests of twigs. He built a model airplane.* *verb,* **built.**

**bush** (bush), **1** a woody plant smaller than a tree, often with many branches starting from or near the ground. **2** open forest or wild land. *noun, plural* **bush·es.**

bush
(def. 1)

**329**

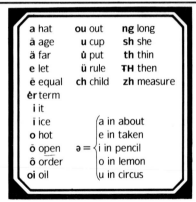

| | | |
|---|---|---|
| a hat | ou out | ng long |
| ā age | u cup | sh she |
| ä far | u̇ put | th thin |
| e let | ü rule | ᴛʜ then |
| ē equal | ch child | zh measure |
| ėr term | | |
| i it | | |
| ī ice | | a in about |
| o hot | | e in taken |
| ō open | ə = | i in pencil |
| ô order | | o in lemon |
| oi oil | | u in circus |

**bush·el** (bush′əl), **1** a set amount used to measure grain, fruit, vegetables, and other dry things, equal to 4 pecks. **2** a container that holds a bushel. *noun.*

**bus·y** (biz′ē), **1** having plenty to do; working a great deal: *The principal of our school is a busy person.* **2** full of work or activity: *Main Street is a busy place. adjective.*

# C c

canoe

**ca·noe** (kə nü′), a light, narrow boat pointed at both ends and moved with a paddle. *noun.*

**cat·a·logue** (kat′l ôg), a list. Some businesses print catalogues showing pictures and prices of the things that they have to sell. *noun.* Also spelled **catalog,** *plural* **cat·a·logues.**

**cel·er·y** (sel′ər ē), a long, crisp vegetable. Celery is eaten raw or cooked. *noun.*

celery

**cham·pi·on** (cham′pē ən), a person, animal, or thing that wins first place in a game or contest: *a swimming champion.*

**choc·o·late** (chôk′lit *or* chôk′ə lit), **1** a strong, rich food made by roasting and grinding cacao seeds. **2** a drink made of chocolate with hot milk or water and sugar. **3** a candy made of chocolate. *noun.* [The name for the drink was borrowed from a Mexican Spanish word. Spanish settlers got it from the American Indian name for the food.]

**cir·cle** (sėr′kəl), **1** a round line. Every point on a circle is equally distant from the center. **2** to go around in a circle: *The plane circled until the fog lifted and it was able to land.* **1** *noun,* **2** *verb,* **cir·cled**.

coin

**coin** (koin), a type of money; change. Pennies, nickels, dimes, and quarters are coins. *noun.*

**con·trol** (kən trōl′), to have power or authority over; direct: *The driver controls the car. verb,* **con·trols**.

cook
(def. 1)

**cook** (kŭk), **1** to prepare food by using heat. Boiling, frying, broiling, roasting, and baking are forms of cooking. **2** to undergo cooking; be cooked: *Let the meat cook slowly. verb.*

**cre·ate** (krē āt′), to make a thing which has not been made before; cause to be: *Composers create music. verb.*

**cur·i·os·i·ty** (kyŭr′ē os′ə tē), **1** an eager wish to know: *Curiosity got the better of me, and I opened the unmarked box.* **2** a strange, or rare object: *One of the curiosities we saw on our trip to the museum was a spoon made from the horn of a deer. noun, plural* **cur·i·os·i·ties**.

# D d

**dan·ger·ous** (dān′jər əs), likely to cause harm; not safe; risky: *Shooting off firecrackers can be dangerous. adjective.*

**dare** (der *or* dar) **1** to be bold; be bold enough: *The children dared to enter the haunted house.* **2** to challenge: *I dare you to jump over the puddle. verb.*

**daugh·ter** (dô′tər), a female child. A girl or woman is the daughter of her mother and father. *noun.*

**de·li·cious** (di lish′əs), very pleasing or satisfying; delightful, especially to the taste or smell: *The birthday cake we had at the party was very delicious. adjective.*

| a hat | ou out | ng long |
|-------|--------|---------|
| ā age | u cup | sh she |
| ä far | ù put | th thin |
| e let | ü rule | TH then |
| ē equal | ch child | zh measure |
| ėr term | | |
| i it | | |
| ī ice | | a in about |
| o hot | | e in taken |
| ō open | ə = | i in pencil |
| ô order | | o in lemon |
| oi oil | | u in circus |

**de·sign** (di zīn′), **1** a drawing, plan, or sketch made to serve as a pattern from which to work: *The design showed how to build the machine.* **2** the arrangement of details, form, and color of something: *We chose a wallpaper design with tan and white stripes. noun.*

**de·ter·mined** (di tėr′mənd), firm; with the mind made up: *Her determined look showed that she had decided. adjective.*

**dic·tion·ar·y** (dik′shə ner′ē), a book that explains the words of a language. It is arranged alphabetically. You can use a dictionary to find out what a word means, how to spell it, or how to say it. *noun.*

**dif·fi·cult** (dif′ə kult), **1** hard to do or understand: *Arithmetic is difficult for some pupils.* **2** hard to deal with or get along with; not easy to please: *My cousins are difficult and always want their own way. adjective.*

**dis·cov·er** (dis kuv′ər), to find out; see or learn of for the first time: *Madame Curie discovered the element radium. verb,* **dis·cov·ered.**

**dress** (dres), **1** a piece of clothing sometimes worn by women and girls. A dress is a top and skirt made as one piece or sewed together. **2** clothes; clothing: *They went to the dance in formal dress. noun.*

dress
(def. 1)

# E e

**ear** (ir), the part of the body with which people and animals hear. *noun.*

**easy** (ē′zē), not hard to do or get: *Easy work is quickly done. adjective.*
**easier**

**e·lec·tric·i·ty** (i lek′tris′ə tē), a form of energy that can produce light, heat, or movement. *noun.*

**e·lev·en** (i lev′ən), one more than ten; 11. *noun, adjective.*

**en·er·gy** (en′ər jē), **1** the will to work; vigor: *I was so full of energy that I could not keep still.* **2** the power to work or act; force: *All our energies were used in keeping the fire from spreading. noun, plural,* **en·er·gies.**

**eve·ning** (ēv′ning), the time between sunset and bedtime: *We spent the evening watching TV. noun.*

**e·vent** (i vent′), **1** a major happening; *The discovery of America was a great event.* **2** an item or contest in a program of sports: *Running a mile was the last event. noun.*

**ex·cept** (ek sept′), leaving out; other than: *He works every day except Sunday. preposition.*

# F f

**fa·mous** (fā′məs), very well known; noted: *The famous singer was greeted by a large crowd. adjective.*

**fan·cy** (fan′sē), not plain or simple; decorated: *a fancy dinner for guests. She wore a fancy dress to the party. adjective.*

**fas·ten** (fas′n), to tie, lock, or hold together in any way: *fasten a door. He fastened his seat belt. verb,* **fas·tened.**

**fa·vor·ite** (fā′vər it), liked better than others: *Blue is my favorite color. adjective.*

**feath·ers** (fe′ərz), the light, thin growths that cover a bird's skin. *Because feathers are soft and light, they are used to fill pillows. noun.*

feathers

**fierce** (firs), **1** wild, scary: *A wounded lion can be fierce.* **2** very great or strong; *fierce anger, a fierce wind. adjective.*

| | | |
|---|---|---|
| **a** hat | **ou** out | **ng** long |
| **ā** age | **u** cup | **sh** she |
| **ä** far | **u̇** put | **th** thin |
| **e** let | **ü** rule | **TH** then |
| **ē** equal | **ch** child | **zh** measure |
| **ėr** term | | |
| **i** it | | |
| **ī** ice | ⎧ **a** in about | |
| **o** hot | ⎪ **e** in taken | |
| **ō** open | **ə** = ⎨ **i** in pencil | |
| **ȯ** order | ⎪ **o** in lemon | |
| **oi** oil | ⎩ **u** in circus | |

**fig·ure** (fig′yər), a form or shape: *I could see the figure of a woman behind the window shade. noun.*

**figure skate**, to ice skate tracing shapes on the ice. *verb.*

**fire** (fīr), the flame, heat, and light caused by something burning. *noun.*

**flee** (flē), to run away: *The robbers fled when the alarm sounded. verb,* **fled.**

**freeze** (frēz), **1** to harden by cold; turn into a solid: *The rain froze into ice on the road.* **2** to make or become very cold: *We will freeze at the football game if we don't wear warm clothes. verb.*

**fruit** (früt) **1** a juicy or fleshy product of a tree, bush, shrub, or vine, often sweet and good to eat. Apples, oranges, bananas, and berries are fruit. **2** the part of a plant where the seeds are. Pea pods, acorns, and grains of wheat are fruits. *noun.*

fruit (def. 1)

# G g

**got·ten** (got′n), **1** past tense of get. **2** came to have; obtained; *Have you gotten the bike you wanted?* **2** has become: *It has gotten much colder. verb.*

**grand** (grand) **1** large and of fine appearance: *The King and queen had a grand throne. adjective.*

**greet** (grēt), to speak or write to in a friendly, polite way; address in welcome; *She greeted us with a friendly "Hello." verb.*

greet

**grouch** (grouch), a grumbling and complaining person. *noun.*

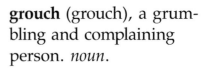

**group** (grüp), a number of persons or things together: *A group of children were playing tag.* noun.

**gruff** (gruf), deep and harsh: *a gruff voice.* adjective.

**grump·y** (grum′pē), bad-tempered; grouchy: *I went to bed late last night and woke up this morning feeling grumpy.* adjective, **grump·i·er, grump·i·est.**

**guard** (gärd), a person who watches over, takes care of, keeps safe, or defends someone or something: *The guard in the library checked everyone's bags.* noun.

guard

**guest** (gest), a person who is received and entertained at another's house; visitor. *noun.*

# H h

**half·way** (haf′wā′), **1** half the way; in the middle: *The rope reached only halfway around the tree.* **2** not completely: *a job that is halfway finished.* adverb.

**ham·mock** (ham′ək), a hanging bed or couch made of rope or canvas. *noun.*

hammock

**hap·pi·ness** (hap′ē nis), the state of being happy or pleased, gladness: *I was filled with happiness when I heard the good news.* noun.

**hawk** (hôk), a hunting bird with a strong, hooked beak, and large bent claws. *noun.*

hawk

**health·y** (hel′thē), **1** being well or not sick; free from illness of any kind: *a healthy baby.* **2** good for the health. *adjective,* **health·i·er.**

**heav·y** (hev′ē), hard to lift or carry. *adjective,* **heav·i·er.**

**he'd** (hēd), **1** he had. *He'd gone fishing last weekend.* **2** he would. *He'd like to see the movie.*

| a hat | ou out | ng long |
|-------|--------|---------|
| ā age | u cup | sh she |
| ä far | ů put | th thin |
| e let | ü rule | ᴛʜ then |
| ē equal | ch child | zh measure |
| ėr term | | |
| i it | | |
| ī ice | | (a in about |
| o hot | | e in taken |
| ō open | ə = | i in pencil |
| ô order | | o in lemon |
| oi oil | | u in circus |

howl

**howl** (houl), to give a long, loud, sad cry: *Our dog often howls at night. The winter winds howled around our cabin.* verb, **howled.**

**hum** (hum), **1** to make a steady, murmuring sound like that of a bee or of a spinning top: *The sewing machine hums busily.* **2** to sing with closed lips, not sounding words: *She was humming a tune.* verb.

# I i

**i·cy** (ī′sē), **1** like ice; very cold: *icy fingers.* **2** covered with ice; slippery: *The car skidded on the icy street.* adjective, **i·ci·er, i·ci·est.**

**i·mag·i·na·tion** (i maj′ə nā′shən), an im-agining; ability to form pictures in the mind. A poet, artist, or inventor must have imagination to create new things or ideas. noun.

**i·mag·ine** (i maj′ən), to form a picture of in the mind; have an idea: *The girl likes to imagine herself a doctor. We can hardly imagine life without electricity.* verb.

**im·por·tant** (im pôrt′nt), meaning much; having value or great effect: *important business, an important occasion.* adjective.

**in·spi·ra·tion** (in′spə rā′shən), **1** the effect of thought and strong feelings on actions, especially on good actions: *Some people get inspiration from nature.* **2** a sudden, great idea. noun.

**in·ter·est·ed** (in′tər ə stid), showing a feeling of wanting to know; see, do, own, or share in; curious about: *An interested crowd gathered at the monkey cage at the zoo.* adjective.

**isle** (īl), **1** a small island. **2** an island. *noun.*

**it·self** (it self′), **1** a form of *it* used to make a statement stronger: *The land itself is worth the money, without the house.* **2** a form used instead of *it*, *him*, or *her* in cases like: *The horse tripped and hurt itself.* *pronoun.*

# J j

jail

**jail** (jāl), a building for persons awaiting trial or being punished for some small crime. *noun.*

**juice** (jüs), the liquid part of fruits, vegetables, and meats: *lemon juice.* *noun.*

# L l

**let·ter** (let′ər), a written or printed message: *He told me about his trip in a letter. noun.*

**li·brar·i·an** (lī brer′ē ən), **1** a person who works in a library. *noun.*

**lone·ly** (lōn′lē), **1** feeling oneself alone and wishing for company or friends: *He was lonely while his brother was away.* **2** without many people: *a lonely road. adjective.*

# M m

**mask** (mask), **1** a covering to hide, protect, or change the look of the face. *noun.*

mask

**ma·ter·i·al** (mə tir′ē əl), **1** what a thing is made of: *Wood and steel are building materials.* **2** a fabric; cloth: *I chose a colorful material for the bedspread. noun, plural* **ma·ter·i·als.**

**men·tion** (men′shən), to speak about: *I mentioned your idea to my friend. verb.*

**mid·dle** (mid′l), **1** the point or part that is equally distant from each end or side; center. **2** halfway between; in the center; at the same distance from either end or side: *the middle house in the row.* **1** *noun,* **2** *adjective.*

| a hat | ou out | ng long |
|-------|--------|---------|
| ā age | u cup | sh she |
| ä far | u̇ put | th thin |
| e let | ü rule | ᴛ𝗛 then |
| ē equal | ch child | zh measure |
| ėr term | | |
| i it | | |
| ī ice | | a in about |
| o hot | | e in taken |
| ō open | ə = | i in pencil |
| ô order | | o in lemon |
| oi oil | | u in circus |

**mill** (mil), a building containing a machine for grinding grain into flour or meal. *noun.*

**mix·ture** (miks′chər), **1** a mixing; a putting together: *The mixture of the paints took ten minutes.* **2** something that has been mixed or combined: *The cake is made from a mixture of butter, milk, flour, and eggs. noun.*

**mo·ment** (mō′mənt), **1** a very short space of time; instant: *I'll be with you in a moment.* **2** a particular point of time: *I started the very moment I got your note. noun.*

**mon·ey** (mun′ē), coins or paper notes for the purpose of paying for things. *noun.*

**month** (munth), one of the twelve parts of time into which a year is divided. *noun.*

**mudd·led** (mud′ld), mixed up; confused: *The team failed to score because the signals were muddled. adjective.*

**muf·fler** (muf′lər), a wrap or scarf worn around the neck for warmth. *noun.*

muffler

**mu·sic** (myü′zik), **1** the art of making sounds that are beautiful, and putting them together into pleasing arrangements. *noun.*

# N n

**nat·ur·al** (nach′ər əl), **1** produced by nature; coming in the normal course of events: *natural feelings, a natural death.* **2** not made by human beings: *Coal and oil are natural products. adjective.*

**no·bod·y** (nō′bod′ē), **1** no one; no person: *Nobody would help me. pronoun*

# Glossary

**north** (nôrth), **1** the direction to which a compass needle points; direction to the right as one faces the setting sun. **2** the north; farther north: *Drive north for the next mile.* **1** *noun,* **2** *adjective.*

# O o

**ob·ject** (ob′jikt), something that can be seen or touched; thing: *What is that object by the fence? noun, plural* **ob·jects.**

**op·e·rate** (op′ə rāt′), **1** to be at work; run: *The machines operate night and day.* **2** to keep at work; run: *to operate an elevator. verb.*

**o·range** (ôr′inj), **1** a color that is made from yellow and red. **2** having this color. **1** *noun,* **2** *adjective.*

# P p

**par·ent** (per′ənt *or* par′ənt), **1** a father or mother. **2** any living thing that has children. *noun.*

**pat·i·o** (pat′ē ō), **1** an inner yard open to the sky. Patios are found especially in houses built in Spanish or Spanish-American style. **2** a porch for outdoor eating. *noun.*

patio
(def. 1)

**per·haps** (pər haps′), it may be; possibly: *Perhaps the letter will come. adverb.*

**pet·ti·coat** (pet′ē kōt), a skirt sometimes worn beneath a dress or outer skirt by women, common in pioneer days. *noun.*

**plains** (plānz), flat stretches of land: *Cattle wandered over the western plains. noun.*

**plead** (plēd), **1** to ask sincerely; beg: *When the rent was due, the poor family pleaded for more time. verb,* **pleaded.**

**pleas·ure** (plezh′ər), **1** a feeling of being pleased; delight; joy: *His pleasure in the gift was obvious.* **2** something that pleases; causes of joy or delight: *It would be a pleasure to see you again. noun.*

| | | |
|---|---|---|
| a hat | ou out | ng long |
| ā age | u cup | sh she |
| ä far | ů put | th thin |
| e let | ü rule | ᴛн then |
| ē equal | ch child | zh measure |
| ėr term | | |
| i it | | |
| ī ice | | a in about |
| o hot | | e in taken |
| ō open | ə = | i in pencil |
| ô order | | o in lemon |
| oi oil | | u in circus |

**plop** (plop), to fall or cause to fall: *She plopped her books down on the table. verb,* **plopped.**

**pole** (pōl), a long, slender piece of wood or the like: *a telephone pole, a totem pole. noun.*

pounce
(def. 1)

**pounce** (pouns), **1** to jump suddenly and seize: *The cat pounced upon the mouse.* **2** a sudden swoop. **1** *verb,* **2** *noun.* [*Pounce* comes from an earlier English word meaning "talon" or "claw." To *pounce* originally meant "to seize with the talons."]

**proof** (prüf), a way or means of showing something is true. *Is what you say a guess or have you proof? noun.*

**prop·er·ly** (prop′ər lē), in a fitting, or correct, manner. *We were told to behave properly at the party. adverb.*

**prove** (prüv), **1** to show that a thing is true and right: *Prove your own statement.* **2** to turn out; be found to be: *The book proved interesting. verb.*

**pro·vide** (prə vīd′), **1** to give what is needed or wanted; supply; furnish: *The school provided cheap lunches for students.* **2** to state as a rule: *Our club's rules provide that dues must be paid monthly. verb.*

**pur·ple** (pėr′pəl), **1** a dark color that is made from red and blue. **2** having this color: *purple grapes.* **1** *noun,* **2** *adjective.*

# R r

**re·al·ize** (rē′ə līz), **1** to understand clearly: *I realize how hard you worked.* **2** to make real: *Her uncle's gift made it possible for her to realize the dream of going to medical school. verb.*

**rea·son** (rē′zn), **1** a cause: *I have my reasons for doing it this way.* **2** an explaining; explanation: *What is your reason for being so late? noun.*

**re·cord** (ri kôrd′), to put into writing or some other permanent form to use later on: *Record what the speaker says. We record history in books. verb.*

# S s

**scat·ter** (skat′ər), **1** to throw here and there; sprinkle: *I scattered seeds on the grass to feed the birds. verb,* **scat·tered.**

**sci·en·tist** (sī′ən tist), a person especially trained in the facts and laws of such fields of study as biology, chemistry, mathematics, geology, and astronomy. *noun, plural* **sci·en·tists.**

scissors

**scis·sors** (siz′ərz), a tool or instrument for cutting that has two sharp blades. *noun plural or singular.*

**scrap** (skrap), a small piece; little bit; small part left over: *The cook gave some scraps of meat to the dog. noun.*

**se·cret** (sē′krit), something that others are kept from knowing: *The plan is a secret. noun.*

**ser·i·ous** (sir′ē əs), **1** thoughtful, grave: *a serious face.* **2** not fooling; sincere. **3** important, needing thought: *Choice of one's life work is a serious matter. adjective.* **ser·i·ous·ly,** *adverb.*

**serve** (sėv), **1** to bring food to: *The waiter served us.* **2** to put food or drink on the table: *The waitress served the soup. verb.*

**sev·er·al** (sev′ər əl), more than two or three but not many; some; a few: *He gained several pounds. adjective, noun.*

**sew 1** work with a needle and thread. **2** fasten with stitches. *Sewing the socks took a long time. verb,* **sew·ing.**

| a hat | ou out | ng long |
|---|---|---|
| ā age | u cup | sh she |
| ä far | ů put | th thin |
| e let | ü rule | ᴛʜ then |
| ē equal | ch child | zh measure |
| ėr term | | |
| i it | | |
| ī ice | | (a in about |
| o hot | | e in taken |
| ō open | ə = | i in pencil |
| ô order | | o in lemon |
| oi oil | | u in circus |

shadow

**shad·ow** (shad′ō), **1** the shade made by some person, animal, or thing. **2 shadows**, darkness; partly shaded: *There was someone lurking in the shadows.* *noun.*

**shell** (shel), the hard outside covering of certain animals. Clams, turtles, and beetles all have shells. *noun.*

**shoul·der** (shōl′dər), the part of the body to which an arm, foreleg, or wing is attached. *noun.*

**sil·ver** (sil′vər), **1** a shining white valuable metal that is a chemical element. *The knives and forks were made of silver.* **2** coins made of this or a similar similar metal: *a pocketful of silver. noun.*

**sock·et** (sok′it), a hollow part or piece for receiving and holding something. A candlestick has a socket for a candle. A light bulb is screwed into a socket. Your eyes are set in sockets. *noun.*

**soft** (sôft), **1** gentle; kind; tender: *Use a soft touch when you pet the young kitten.* **2** quiet: *We heard a soft whisper from the next room. adjective.* **soft·ly**, *adverb.*

**sol·emn** (sol′əm), **1** serious; grave; earnest: *a solemn voice. He gave his solemn promise to do better. adjective.* **sol·emn·ly**, *adverb.*

**spar·kle** (spär′kəl), to shine; glitter; flash: *The jewels in the crown sparkled. verb.*

**splot** (splot), informal for **splotch**; a large, messy spot; splash. *noun.*

spot

**spot** (spot), to pick out; find out; recognize: *She spotted her sister in the crowd. My history teacher* *spotted every mistake in last research report.* verb, **spot ·ted.**

**sprin·kle** (spring′kəl), **1** to scatter in drops or tiny bits: *I sprinkled sand on the icy sidewalk so people wouldn't slip and fall.* **2** to spray or cover with small drops: *She sprinkled the flowers with water.* verb.

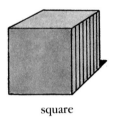

square

**square** (skwer), **1** a figure with four equal sides and four right angles. **2** anything having this shape. *The quilt was made with squares of cloth.* noun, plural **squares.**

**stat·ue** (stach′ü), a likeness of a person or animal carved in stone or wood, cast plaster, or modeled in clay or wax: *Nearly every city has a statue of some famous person.* noun.

**stead·y** (sted′ē), **1** changing very little; regular: *steady speed, a steady gain in value.* **2** firmly fixed; firm; not swaying or shaking: *This post is steady as a rock.* adjective.

**stem** (stem), **1** the main supporting part of a plant above the ground. The stem holds up the branches. The trunk of a tree is a stem. **2** the part of a flower, a fruit, or a leaf that joins it to the plant or tree. **3** anything like the stem of a plant. *the stem of a wine glass, the stem of a pipe.* noun.

**stitch** (stich), **1** one complete movement of a threaded needle in sewing: *Take short stitches so the seam will be strong.* **2** one complete movement in knitting, etc. **3** a loop of thread or yarn made by a stitch: *Rip out these long stitches. The doctor took the stitches out of my cut.* noun, plural **stitch·es.**

stoop

**stoop** (stüp), to bend forward: *I stooped to pick up the money.* verb, **stooped.**

**stran·ger** (strā′jər), **1** a person not known, seen, or heard of before: *She is a stranger to us.* **2** a person or thing new to a place: *I am a stranger in New York.* noun.

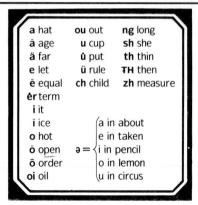

| | | |
|---|---|---|
| a hat | ou out | ng long |
| ā age | u cup | sh she |
| ä far | ů put | th thin |
| e let | ü rule | ŦH then |
| ē equal | ch child | zh measure |
| ėr term | | |
| i it | | |
| ī ice | | a in about |
| o hot | | e in taken |
| ō open | ə = | i in pencil |
| ô order | | o in lemon |
| oi oil | | u in circus |

**stream** (strēm), **1** a flow of water in a channel or bed. Small rivers and large brooks are both called streams. **2** any steady flow: *a stream of lava, noun.*

**stroll** (strōl), **1** to take a quiet walk for pleasure; walk: *We strolled through the park after dinner.* **2** a slow walk: *We went for a stroll in the park.* **1** *verb,* **2** *noun.*

**stuff** (stuf), **1** what a thing is made of; material: *She bought some white stuff for curtains.* **2** belongings; goods: *She was told to move her stuff out of the room. noun.*

**sub·ject** (sub′jikt), something thought about, dis-cussed, or studied; topic: *The subject for our writing lesson is "An Exciting Moment." noun.*

**sud·den** (sud′n), **1** not expected; quick; rapid: *The people on the island were not prepared for the sudden storm. adjective.*
**sud·den·ly,** unexpectedly; quickly; rapidly: *The storm came up suddenly. The cat suddenly jumped at a mouse. adverb.*

**sup·posed** (sə pōzd′), considered as possible or probable; accepted as true: *The supposed beggar was really a prince. adjective.*

**sur·round** (sə round′), to shut in on all sides; extend around; enclose: *A very high fence made of huge bricks surrounded the field. verb,* **sur·round·ed.**

**switch** (swich), a thing by which electricity is turned on or off: *It's getting dark—please flip the switch and turn on the lights. noun.*

switch

# T t

**ta·ble** (tā′bəl), a thing having a smooth, flat top on legs. *noun.*

telephone
(def. 1)

**tel·e·phone** (tel′ə fōn), **1** an instrument for talking between distant points over wires by means of electricity. **2** to talk through a telephone; **1** *noun,* **2** *verb.* [*Telephone* was formed from two Greek words meaning "far off," and "sound" or "voice."]

**test** (test), try out: *The teacher tested our reading skills. verb,* **tested.**

**though** (ŦHō), **1** in spite of the fact that: *Though it was raining, we went on the trip.* **2** however: *I am sorry for our fight; you began it, though.* **1** *conjunction,* **2** *adverb.*

**thou·sand** (thou′znd), ten hundred; 1,000. *noun, adjective.* **thousands,** more than one thousand; a great many.

**thump** (thump), to strike with something thick and heavy; pound: *She thumped the table with her fist. verb,* **thumping.**

**touch** (tuch), **1** to put the hand or some other part of the body on and feel: *I touched the kitten. verb.*

**twist** (twist), **1** to turn with a winding move-ment: *I twisted the cap off the jar.* **2** to wind togeth-er; wind. *verb.*

**type** (tīp), a kind, sort, or group alike in some way: *She is the type of person I like, kind and friendly. noun.*

# U u

**un·cle** (ung′kəl), **1** a brother of one's father or mother. *noun.*

**un·com·fort·a·ble** (un kum′fər tə bəl), **1** causing mild pain: *an uncomfort-able chair.* **2** causing an uneasy feeling: *His stares made me feel uncomfortable. adjective.*

| a hat | ou out | ng long |
|---|---|---|
| ā age | u cup | sh she |
| ä far | ů put | th thin |
| e let | ü rule | TH then |
| ē equal | ch child | zh measure |
| ėr term | | |
| i it | | |
| ī ice | | (a in about |
| o hot | | e in taken |
| ō open | ə = | i in pencil |
| ô order | | o in lemon |
| oi oil | | u in circus |

**u·su·al·ly** (yü′zhü ə lē), commonly: *We usually eat dinner at six.* adverb.

# V v

**val·u·a·ble** (val′yü ə bəl), **1** merit having value: *valuable information, a valuable friend.* **2** costing much money: *a valuable ring.* adjective.

vegetable
(def. 1)

**vege·ta·ble** (vej′tə bəl *or* vej′ə tə bəl), **1** a plant whose fruit, seeds, leaves, roots, or other parts are used for food: *We grow vegetables such as peas, corn, and beets in our garden.* **2** the part of such a plant which is used for food: *Shall we have broccoli for a vegetable at dinner tonight?* noun.

**ven·ture** (ven′chər), **1** a risky or daring undertaking: *The explorers hoped to find gold on their venture into the wilderness.* **2** to expose to risk or danger: *She ventured her life to rescue me.* **1** *noun,* **2** *verb.*

**vil·lage** (vil′ij), **1** a group of houses, usually smaller than a town. **2** the people of a village: *The whole village came out to see the fire.* noun.

# W w

**wan·der** (won′dər), to move here and there without any special purpose: *We wandered around the fair, looking at displays.* verb. **wan·der·ing,** adjective.

**we're** (wir), we are. We're going to the play on Saturday.

**wob·ble** (wob′əl), **1** to move unsteadily from side to side; shake; tremble: *A baby wobbles when it begins to walk alone.* **2** a wobbling movement. **1** *verb,* **wob·bled; 2** *noun.*

**wom·en** (wim′ən), more than one woman. *noun.*

**worth** (wẻrth), **1** good or important enough for; *That book is worth reading.* **2** equal in value to: *This* book is worth five dollars. *preposition.*

# Y y

**young** (yung), in the early part of life or growth; not old: *A puppy is a young dog. adjective.*